RADICAL
CHURCH PLANTING

RADICAL CHURCH PLANTING

by

Roger Ellis

&

Roger Mitchell

(with chapters by
Roger Forster and Sandy Millar)

CROSSWAY BOOKS
Cambridge

Cover Design by Payne Butler, Newport Pagnell

ISBN 1-85684-036-0

Production in England for
CROSSWAY BOOKS
Kingfisher House, 7 High Green, Great Shelford,
Cambridge CB2 1SG by
Stephen Ayres Bureau, 3 Clifton Court, Cambridge CB1 4BN
Printed by
Cox & Wyman Ltd, Reading, Berkshire

ACKNOWLEDGEMENTS

For both of us Church Planting has involved learning from success and failure in the context of our relationships. This whole book was born out of the growing friendship we have enjoyed. Indeed, without the friendship, sacrifice and committment of many others around us we would have little of significance to communicate.

This book is dedicated to those in Ichthus, Revelation and the Pioneer network who have taught and cared for us whilst giving themselves wholeheartedly, often at great personal cost, to the work of God.

I'd like to thank Gerald Coates, Steve Clifford and Martin Scott for their friendshipand influence. Margaret, my wife is a wonderful partner both in marriage and leadership. Chris Seaton and Mike Morris, who have expanded, developed and turned much of my vision into reality. James Sharp, Adam Ashworth and Ian Stewart - true sons in the faith. Malc and Kathy Garda - significant people and great friends. Also to ALL our leadership team which includes people like Graham and Liza Cooke, Simon and Laraine Fenner, Mike and Allison Wilkerson, Malc and Pam Herrington, Jeff and Kay Lucas, Murray Jacobs and Pete and Nikki Gilbert. I take my hat off to you all!

Roger Ellis

Special acknowledgments to my wife Sue, Roger and Faith Forster and other members of the Ichthus Leadership and team for all they have taught me over the years, and to the indefatigable Marjie Sutton, the best PA in the world'

Roger Mitchell

CONTENTS

FOREWORD
BY
GERALD COATES

For churches in our Pioneer network *Radical Church Planting* will be "essential" reading.

Radical Church Planting. What does that mean? The Oxford Dictionary informs us that there are two words, both identically pronounced. *Radicle* is a noun – and describes the part of a seed that develops into the root. The more widely used *Radical* is an adjective and describes "going to" or "being the root", also "inherent, essential".

Charismatic evangelical New Churches (House Churches) are the fastest growing wing of the church at present. But as my colleague John Noble has observed, statistics can only tell you what has happened, they are a hopeless guide to assessing the future. Humility can give way to arrogance, wisdom to triumphalism. History is full of "God exalting the humble" soon followed by "how are the mighty fallen"!

"Church planting", a few years ago, was a dirty couplet. Now evangelical Anglicans, Methodists, Baptists, Pentecostals, Salvationists, Independent evangelical churches and the New Churches, are all planning substantial increases within their groupings and streams, mainly through Church planting. Strategies are emerging for the inner city, suburbia and rural areas. Why? Because as long as I have lived – some 47 years – church attendance has been at times in steady and at other times, rapid decline. Denominationalism lost a million members in the 1970s and around half a million in the 1980s. Decline is still the pattern for the church as a whole, though conservative evangelical churches and particularly charismatic evangelical churches have been and will continue to enjoy health and numerical growth.

My greatest fear, nevertheless, is that many churches, who the status quo would call "radical" are far from it. Many have changed their liturgy, but have remained the same. Exchanging old hymns with Shakespearian language for Kendrick, Bowater or Richards is not necessarily radical. Shelving one hour services for two hour meetings need not be radical. Ditching the organ for a soft rock band need not be radical either. We can still be looking in and down rather than up and out. This simply purifies the lump, consolidates or makes public times together more enjoyable – but in the words of Os Guinness can make us "Privately engaging but socially irrelevant".

It is my hope that this book will help change all of that. In our Pioneer network of churches, we have a simple theological framework that even the most uneducated believer can grasp. We should not be surprised that this framework and emphasis come from Jesus the Radical. Apostolic and prophetic ministry should be interpreted in the light and teachings of Jesus Christ himself. Our framework emphasises:

1.   A policy of co-operation. We draw this from Jesus' prayer recorded for us in John 17. When he prays "That they may be one" he gives the reason. "That the world may know" that the father has sent the son into the world. As Christians we are called to demonstrate our love for one another.

2.   Networking our "world" with the Gospel. (Mt 24.14). Jesus explains that when the good news about the Kingdom of God has been lived out and preached in every people group "then the end will come". There is no greater service we could do for the majority of people groups in the world than to bring an end to the darkness and depression, abuse and tragedies that overtake entire communities. Hunger and thirst dominate some nations. Fear and paranoia haunt city streets, our villages, indeed entire people groups. So each of us has a responsibility to help build communities in every people group, who can be good news and share that good news with those around them. This is church planting, radical church that goes to the root of our failure to communicate the Gospel to cultures within our culture.

The 1970s and 1980s saw churches relating on the basis of their ecclesiology – that is, the way we "do" church: charismatic or non-charismatic, traditional or informal, one man ministry or male/female leadership team. I want to suggest that the next decade will see a major shift in terms of how we relate. Leaders and their churches are going to find the togetherness based not on their ecclesiology but on eschatology – end time issues. Taking the Gospel to every people group in a city, town or village will harness our energies and enable us to set corporate goals. Divided armies don't win battles.

This new spirit of co-operation, networking our nations with the Gospel, summed up in John 17 and Matthew 24 will "hasten" the coming of our King. He is not returning for a battered bride, a ramshackle building of a church in hiding, but a people who with a policy of co-operation are seeking to network their worlds, and the people groups within them, with the good news about Jesus.

Social action, being salt and light in the so-called secular world, up-front evangelism, prayer and praise out on the streets, are all a part of the same story – the same drama – to confront the powers of darkness, to expose them for what they are and in the name of Jesus to invade hell with heaven. There is enough hell in homes and schools, hospitals and business premises for us to take up the challenge to take a little bit of heaven wherever we go.

This book is distinguished by the fact that its two main authors, (friends of mine) are actually *doing* what they are talking about. They do not sit in the ivory tower of the study, Bible college or pastor's sanctuary, unhinged from reality. The important chapters written by Roger Forster and Sandy Millar (again friends of mine), one from a New Church and another from an Anglican tradition enrich the book even further with their theological perspectives and practical experience.

My prayer is that this publication will become a resource for all church planters in the future and for those seeking to bring radical change rather than cosmetic renewal to the church.

Gerald Coates
Team Leader Pioneer. Surrey

PART 1

FOUNDATIONS OF CHURCH PLANTING

CHAPTER 1

UPON THIS ROCK

The way God works things out is a constant source of wonder to me. I first learned Christian ministry and evangelism, the proper functions of church, by travelling about the United Kingdom, involved in all kinds of evangelistic projects and missions. These were led by a variety of experienced evangelists, one of whom, Roger Forster, I ended up training alongside full time. I worked with children, teenagers and adults in schools, colleges and universities, among all kinds of people both middle income and poor.

When eventually a group of Christians suggested that we worked out what we'd been teaching and experiencing in a more local context, we were glad. It seemed at the time that the old itinerating model was inadequate. We needed church to give solidity and integrity to the work we'd been doing. It even seemed that the itinerant, one night, one weekend or sometimes week-long 'stands' were an unbiblical approach to the work of the kingdom. But now, in retrospect, I am excited to see that something quite different was happening. God was preparing us for pioneer church planting. The only way to do that was Jesus' way.

Jesus' way of church planting

Jesus' way of training church planters was by putting together an embryonic leadership team with whom he travelled around Judea and Galilee, to whom he taught the principles of his kingdom on the job, and who were effectively the first expression of his church. I realise now that what we were doing was church too. As Jesus said to Peter as he got to know him on those journeys of theirs, 'Upon this rock I will build my church' (Mt 16:18). Which is precisely what he did, of course. Within a three- to four-year period Jesus trained a team of leaders ready to win, mobilise and equip thousands of men and women in divine partnership with the Holy Spirit, beginning with the church at Jerusalem and spreading out over all the earth.

Now although I for one failed to realise it at the time, what Jesus was doing was teaching us church planting principles first hand. Church is not a static local religious institution or club, but a dynamic, progressive movement of men and women in partnership with Jesus by the Holy Spirit, sent out to teach and demonstrate the reality of the kingdom both by travelling teams and by the establishing of local resource bases, all over the earth. It may not be a definition we are used to, or sit comfortably with in the contemporary Christian scene, but it seems to be what Jesus was doing.

The basics of faith

Now as Christians we presumably require no convincing that Jesus is the Word of God incarnate. God in the flesh. 'He who has seen Me has seen the Father' (Jn 14:9); 'I am the way, and the truth, and the life...' (Jn 14:6). I cannot fault the assumption that as well as revealing what God is like, and what we ought to be like, he shows us how to continue the work he began. He has dealt with sin and Satan so that we can receive the Holy Spirit and get on with his work. Our definitions and methods must be based on him. With this presupposition in place we are in the position to take a closer look at what Jesus taught Peter and the rest of his team about church on the road to Caesarea Philippi.

He said to them, 'But who do you say that I am?' And Simon Peter answered and said, 'You are the Christ, the Son of the living God.' And Jesus answered and said to him, 'Blessed are you, Simon Barjonah, because flesh and blood did not reveal this to you, but My Father who is in heaven. And I also say to you that you are Peter, and upon this rock I will build My church; and the gates of Hades shall not overpower it. I will give you the keys of the kingdom of heaven; and whatever you shall bind on earth shall have been bound in heaven, and whatever you shall loose on earth shall have been loosed in heaven' (Mt 16: 15-19).

This incident provides the first mention of church in the New Testament and is one of only two occasions on which Jesus taught about it. The other occasion occurred shortly afterwards and emphasises the absolute necessity of true and forgiving relationships if church is to survive (Mt 18:15-17). These two passages which contain Jesus' direct teaching on the nature of church must be held as central and foundational if we are to be properly Christian in our church-planting principles and methods. The reference in Matthew 18 has to do with preserving church once we have it.

The vital statements on the road to Caesarea Philippi are definitive of what church is and what church is for. We can sum them up as follows: two statements about what church *is* – it is based on revelation and progressive discipleship; and two statements about what church is *for* – it is for displacing the powers of death and unlocking the kingdom of heaven.

We are going to look at these first statements more closely.

1. Revelation

In reply to Peter's confession, 'Thou art the Christ, the Son of the living God,' Jesus responded, 'Flesh and blood did not reveal this to you, but My Father who is in heaven.' Now this is extremely interesting. Jesus says that his church is founded on those to whom the Father has given a revelation of Jesus. Traditionally, we have tended to assume that a Christian is one

3

to whom Jesus reveals the Father. But here Jesus puts it the other way round.

This makes a lot of sense when you think about it. Jesus *does* reveal the Father to us. Like the bystanders of Peter's day, we and our contemporaries have many different opinions about the identity and personality of God and Jesus. But prolonged exposure to Jesus, like Peter and his colleagues had experienced, penetrates the darkness of our misconceptions and blind spots until we begin to see the Father properly. But once the Father is revealed to us he points directly back to Jesus. 'He is the One who has opened your eyes to me. He is the anointed One. He is my Son, the revelation of my heart.' Or, to put it another way, God is just like Jesus. He is truly 'the God of our Lord Jesus Christ, the Father of glory' (Eph 1:17). Man's biggest problem is a wrong view of God. It is these wrong views that lead to legalistic and false religion, agnosticism and atheism and unbelief in its various forms. It is these views that lead to static or shrinking churches and rob us of our proper church-planting vision and destiny. If we take the Father's word for it and realise that the base-line of church is the heaven-sent revelation that God is just like Jesus, we shall open ourselves up to the divine dynamic which produces true church among us. Then, in turn, living church will be reproduced throughout the earth.

An intensely practical conclusion follows from this which we have proved over and over again in the Ichthus experience of church planting. Our team life must focus on Jesus both in word and spirit. First, this means a determination to be more than just biblical, but to seek for the revelation of Christ in all the Scriptures. Secondly, it involves a commitment to staying with the Spirit by constant worship and obedience because it is the Spirit who reveals Jesus and preserves us from dogmatism and legalism.

Much of contemporary thinking about evangelism and expectations of church life are less than truly Christian. The practice of submitting all biblical interpretation, whether Old Testament or New, to the incarnate Christ of the Gospels will keep us from teaching and practices which hinder the growth and multiplication of church. The habit of interspersing all teaching and evangelism with prayer and worship promotes the flow of the Spirit and facilitates the revelation of Jesus. These have been, in our experience, the ways to unity and success.

2. Discipleship

Most of us will be aware that Peter's name was a special nickname given to him by Jesus when they first met. Peter's original name was Simon, which carried the sense of 'hearing' or 'sound' in its original meaning. His new name, however, signified 'stone' or 'small rock'. The implication of this is obvious from Peter's biography in the Gospels. There was plenty of outward sound and noise coming from the natural Simon. Jesus' intention was to make him into a spiritual rock out of which his church could be built. In the light of this, it is not at all difficult to see why Jesus referred to him by his old name Simon on the road to Caesarea. Through the solid rock of the revelation of Jesus ('petra'), a weak and fleshly Simon could become a rock-solid Peter ('Petros'). Peter well understood this, despite the confusions that have raged over the interpretation of this passage among Christians even to the present day. For in later years, writing in his own epistle, he had this to say: 'The stone which the builders rejected, this became the very corner stone... ' (1 Pet 2:7); 'And coming to Him as to a living stone ... you also, as living stones, are being built up as a spiritual house...' (1 Pet 2:4, 5).

Church, then, is the gathering of people on the basis of the revelation of Jesus, in the light of which they are in the process of being changed into his likeness and becoming the very substance of church. The Apostle Paul puts it like this: 'We all, with unveiled face beholding as in a mirror the glory of the Lord, are being transformed into the same image from glory to glory, just as from the Lord, the Spirit' (2 Cor 3:18).

It follows from this that there are really two frontiers for church planting. One is the whole world out there that needs netting by the church with the good news of the kingdom and local resource bases all over the place. But the other frontier is the internal one of our own hearts which, like Peter's, need continuous transformation by exposure to the revelation of Jesus. Paul rightly says: 'If any man is in Christ, he is a new creature; the old things passed away; behold, new things have come' (2 Cor 5:17). However, this applies to the renewal of our spirits. Our minds and characters, our souls and bodies have then to be submitted to the Holy Spirit, and by exposure to Jesus we are transformed.

Back in the early 1980s I learned a very personal lesson about the need to make progress on this internal frontier. It was in the very early stages of what I would call the second phase of our church planting. The first phase was the planting and consolidation of the original Ichthus congregation. This took the better part of eight years to build from an original sixteen or so people to around four hundred. The second phase began as we reached out to multiply further congregations by taking several house groups in or on the edge of our area and placing a team of initiative-taking mobilising types alongside them.

I was working with one of these teams, focusing on a small estate of mainly high-rise flats where there was considerable physical and spiritual poverty. As we prayed over and got to know the area and its people, we soon realised that words alone were not enough to get through to them. School teachers, politicians and the established church had largely exhausted and devalued that coinage without bringing any real help or meaning. It was obvious that we needed a more biblical evangelism than words alone could bring. Like Jesus and Paul we needed the signs of the kingdom to give validity and integrity to our words:

> 'Jesus was going about all the cities and the villages, teaching in their synagogues, and proclaiming the gospel of the kingdom, and healing every kind of disease and every kind of sickness' (Mt 9:35); 'For I will not presume to speak of anything except what Christ has accomplished through

me, resulting in the obedience of the Gentiles by word and deed, in the power of signs and wonders, in the power of the Spirit' (Rom 15:18-19).

The Lord led us to one particular lady with a chronic eye condition. She had such bad corneal ulcers that one eye had been stitched closed for almost twenty years to alleviate the pain of blinking. The condition was beginning to spread to the other eye. We prayed for that lady in every way possible: at home, in church, standing up, sitting down. We anointed her with oil, laid-on hands and fasted. Finally, God gave me a clear word of knowledge. It was a picture of a Second World War baker's shop with a baker taking bread out of the oven. I knew it was the Second World War because it was like a picture in a modern history book I used to teach from. But the woman had had no experience that related to the picture at all!

For days I tried the picture on people I was attempting to help, on the basis that God does not give you a key that fails to unlock anything! Finally, a young colleague, in some frustration, suggested I tried it on myself. Now it so happens that my father was a baker in the Second World War. Indeed he never went to war precisely because baking was a protected trade. This uncovered me fast. I had always been ashamed as a child that my dad had not been to war. There was little logic in my shame as he had seen plenty of courageous action in the Civil Defence, but it was a deep thing for me as a youngster under pressure from mates and media hype. That one little word opened up whole areas where my personal authority and faith had been undermined. Friends and colleagues ministered the healing power of the cross into those inner frontiers. Faith grew and within a few weeks news came of the woman's extraordinary healing through being picked for a successful experiment with a new laser surgery technique.

Since then a successful congregation has been planted on that estate, which has itself already multiplied into two. But the real significance was in the development of the church planter whose faith has grown to accomplish greater things.

Church planting is about this progressive development of disciples, so we must be extremely careful not to lock each other in to our current experience of Christ. Wonderfully, once we embark together on the church planting process, the need to take on new challenges of vision and practical leadership encourages us to expect each other's characters and gifts to develop and grow. But this does not happen easily unless we understand that church is intended by Jesus to be this kind of outgoing developing organisation rather than a static institution. It involves a progressive view of the development of spiritual gifts and ministries and implies that whatever professional training for ministry a person may or may not have, the essential training must be on the job, as it was for those first apostles.

Paul's teaching on spiritual gifts and ministries bears this out, as we shall see later in this book. This is so wonderfully clear in the ongoing life and experience of Peter. Within a few verses of Jesus' commendation of Peter on the road to Caesarea, Jesus calls Peter Satan! Later he explains: 'Simon, Simon, behold, Satan has demanded permission to sift you like wheat; but I have prayed for you, that your faith may not fail; and you, when once you have turned again, strengthen your brothers' (Lk 22:31-32). And again, after Peter's denial Jesus reaffirms his call to pastor the lost if he truly loves him: 'Tend My lambs ... shepherd My sheep ... tend My sheep' (Jn 21:15-17). And so both Peter and the church grow and develop.

3. Displacing the devil

From Jesus' point of view the church exists to deal with the powers of death and the devil. He says to Peter: 'The powers of death shall not prevail against it.' These powers of death are headed by the devil. The writer to the Hebrews speaks of him plainly as he 'who had the power of death, that is, the devil' (Heb 2:14). John recognises this emphatically in his epistle: 'The Son of God appeared for this purpose, that He might destroy the works of the devil' (1 Jn 3:8).

The church's major responsibility for spiritual warfare has often been ignored or called into question. But if we take Jesus as our example, the conclusion is unequivocal. By resisting and rebuking Satan from a lifestyle of prayer and fasting, and by preaching and demonstrating the good news of the kingdom publicly, Jesus opposed and finally defeated the devil in the cross and resurrection. By the same means, and drawing on Jesus' pioneer victory, the church's task is to engage and defeat him too.

It is important to notice that Jesus didn't wait for the devil to come looking for him, but that the Spirit expressly led him out to encounter the devil. At the very beginning of his ministry he was 'led up by the Spirit into the wilderness to be tempted by the devil' (Mt 4:1). This accords with the metaphor Jesus chose in the Greek of Matthew 16, literally, 'The gates of Hades will not prevail against you.' Sometimes we have portrayed the spiritual battle as the church fending off the devil from a position of passive resistance. But whoever heard of anyone being attacked by a pair of gates? Gates are only a problem when you try to get past them. The church is called to an *offensive* against the devil and his powers.

The temptations of Jesus make it clear that Satan leads a spiritual anti-kingdom utterly opposed to Jesus and his kingdom. Satan's kingdom is rooted in materialism, power lust and status seeking. Through these deathly powers he exerts dominion over individual people: 'Command that these stones become bread' (Mt 4:3), over religious and socio-political institutions like the temple: 'Then the devil took Him into the holy city; and he stood Him on the pinnacle of the temple' (Mt 4:5) and over territory: 'The devil took Him to a very high mountain, and showed Him all the kingdoms of the world, and their glory' (Mt 4:8).

Jesus' life was a glorious counter-attack on the devil and these powers of death. Throughout his ministry he progressively bound Satan's power and he cast out demons until the cross where he cast out Satan himself. He thereby established an impregnable stronghold of heaven on earth in the Holy Spirit, whom he poured out onto the church at Pentecost. It is now the church's task, as the body of Christ in a locality, to follow him until we defeat the enemy and secure

9

our own Pentecost of spiritual breakthrough and multiplication. This is clearly the process of church planting in the New Testament church as we shall see.

4. The keys of the kingdom

There is no point in having keys you can't use to unlock things with. Jesus gives the church the keys to his kingdom. The kingdom of God and the way of Jesus are the same thing. This is clear from Matthew's introduction to John the Baptist. John preached: 'Repent, for the kingdom of heaven is at hand.' Matthew says that this fulfils Isaiah's prophecy, 'The voice of one crying in the wilderness, "make ready the way of the Lord, make His paths straight!"'. (Mt 3:3). This makes no sense unless 'the way of the Lord' and 'the kingdom of heaven' are synonymous. This kingdom can be seen in three main ways in Jesus' life: in his relationship with the King as God his Father, in his relationships with his fellow men and women where all the barriers of race, culture and sex are broken down, and in his relationship with everything else as he works to reconcile all things to himself.

This kingdom way of Jesus is referred to on over eighty separate occasions by Jesus in the Gospel accounts. He views it as present in his own life and ministry, as coming one day at his return, and as given to the church in the Holy Spirit in between times. It is the task of the church to unlock the kingdom of heaven in the present. The kingdom is not the church. It is given to the church which is the agent of the kingdom as Luke records: 'Do not be afraid, little flock, for your Father has chosen gladly to give you the kingdom' (Lk 12:32). Although the kingdom of God is profoundly physical and earthly in its effects, it is altogether spiritual at source. This is why it is interchangeably referred to as the kingdom of heaven. Jesus says of it, 'My kingdom is not of this world. If My kingdom were of this world, then My servants would be fighting' (Jn 18:36).

Paul states clearly, 'The kingdom of God is not eating and drinking, but righteousness and peace and joy in the Holy Spirit' (Rom 14:17). The kingdom, therefore, can only be unlocked by spiritual, supernatural means in the same way as

Jesus unlocked it. These means, as I understand them, are doing the works of the kingdom in the way Jesus did them and binding the devil and his powers in the way Jesus did.

All the kingdom-unlocking actions of Jesus in evangelism are available to the church in the Holy Spirit, who remained on him throughout his life and was given to the church at Pentecost. In God the Father's own words to John the Baptist, 'He upon whom you see the Spirit descending and remaining upon Him, this is the one who baptizes with the Holy Spirit' (Jn 1:33). These are what the gifts of the Spirit are. They are Jesus' way of doing things laid up for us in the Holy Spirit and given to us as he fills and baptises us. The church cannot possibly fulfil its job without them.

But in order to let loose the kingdom of heaven we also need to stop the devil and his kingdom. This is what the prayer of faith is all about. 'And Jesus answered saying to them, "Have faith in God. Truly I say to you, whoever says to this mountain, 'Be taken up and cast into the sea,' and does not doubt in his heart, but believes what he says is going to happen, it shall be granted him"' (Mk 11:22–23). This is what Jesus means when he says, 'Whatever you shall bind on earth shall have been bound in heaven; and whatever you shall loose on earth shall have been loosed in heaven.' Some people have tried to say that these words don't refer to devil-shifting prayer and kingdom-bringing work. But Jesus' usage of the words 'binding' and 'loosing' are invariably in this context. In discussion with the Jewish leaders over how he cast out demons he said 'How can anyone enter a strong man's house and carry off his property, unless he first binds the strong man?' (Mt 12:29). He spoke of the woman, 'a daughter of Abraham ... whom Satan has bound for eighteen long years', being 'released from this bond on the Sabbath day' (Lk 13:16). When asked why the disciples were unsuccessful in dealing with a demon-possessed boy, Jesus replied, 'This kind cannot come out by anything but prayer and fasting' (Mk 9:29).

As the church learns to pray in the faith that binds the devil and looses people, institutions and areas from his power, the room is made to unlock the kingdom of heaven by the operation of spiritual gifts in evangelism and so the work of the church progresses.

CHAPTER 2

THE GOSPEL OF THE KINGDOM

In our first chapter we have gained a perspective on the way in which Jesus gathered the embryonic church as portrayed in the context of the Gospels. It is into this mix that the theme of the kingdom of God is inescapably encountered. Observers have commented that Jesus only ever taught about two things: His Father in heaven and the kingdom of God on earth. Another somewhat ruder commentator concluded after studying the Gospels that Jesus was "obsessed by the kingdom"!

Whichever description is used, it is certain that the teaching of the kingdom is fundamental to Jesus' message and should therefore hold the same place in our theology and life. Unfortunately, in many cases, the church has lost this focus to the degree that as a new Christian I had received what would be considered a 'solid evangelical foundation', yet with no significant reference to the kingdom. To compound this, early perspectives I heard concerning it relegated the kingdom exclusively to the future; a kind of spiritual Windsor Castle descending mysteriously around the time of a 'future millennium'!

Could it be that this lost focus has been a major factor in the limitation and domestication of our understanding of the gospel? It is my contention that before we contemplate the nuts and bolts of church planting, we need to ask questions with regard to the kind of message we are proclaiming and what kind of church we want to reproduce. After this refocusing, quite a few leaders I know have concluded that they would like the churches they plant to be altogether different from the ones they are in! And why not? Many fathers and mothers wish for better things for their children than the struggles, pains and restrictions they themselves have endured to get to where they are in life. If this is to be achieved we need to give careful attention to the 'seeds' we plant and the foundations we lay. An acorn can only ever become an oak, no matter how much we wish otherwise. The purpose of this chapter is to confirm that the gospel of the kingdom is a key seed from which our understanding of church planting should grow. The nature and quality of this seed will dictate the shape, form, size and health of the living organism which is eventually produced.

The centrality of the kingdom

The kingdom of God is not just another model of church, a metaphor for it like the body (Eph 4:12), the household of God, the pillar and foundation of the truth (1 Tim 3:15) or the bride of Christ (Rev 19:7). Neither is it a synonym for church as some would suggest. The idea often purported is that just as the word 'church' (*ekklesia*) signifies our nature as a called-out people with a unique purpose before us, so the kingdom reveals that as a community the church expresses God's rule and reign in its lifestyle.

I would like to suggest that perspectives like these are too limited. Rather, the kingdom of God is far broader and more significant, and while as a church we are to seek it above all things (Mt 6:33), its sphere reaches far beyond our boundaries.

Looking at the New Testament, it seems that the words 'kingdom', 'salvation' and 'eternal life' are used almost interchangeably. In fact the term "the gospel of the kingdom" is used over a dozen times. Commentators are not out of place, therefore, when they describe the kingdom as, "The whole preaching of Jesus Christ and the Apostles," or, "The basic theme Jesus proclaimed." Indeed, one rabbi declared that the kingdom is the "very truth and essence of the law". Clearly, in the light of this, we must be looking to plant churches that embody a kingdom ethos and pulsate with its life. Kingdom churches will refuse to be blinkered by one agenda, be it evangelical, socio-political, denominational or charismatic. They will be caught up with pursuing the reign of God in every area of life and existence.

God's reign breaking in

In using the name King, of Jesus (Rev 19:16), Scripture reveals to us something every pioneer needs to keep in mind. God is not just personal, he is almighty, all-powerful and he reigns. As the advancing church seeks to destroy the work of the enemy (Mt 12:25–29) and bring territory under God's reign, we should remember that fundamentally 'the earth is the Lord's, and everything in it' (Ps 24:1). Also, it is not a dualistic battle between two sides of equal power and authority. Satan has fallen like lightning from heaven and Christ reigns over all things for the church (Eph 1:22). It is not a bad place to start from when church planting!

Further, as Martin Scott observes[2], the biblical words for kingdom are *malkuth* in Hebrew and *basileia* in Greek. The meaning carried by these words is primarily that of 'rule' and 'reign' rather than 'realm'. It is the dynamic breaking in of God, and his activity, rather than a static sphere. Therefore, since the kingdom is God's Holy Spirit activity it cannot be institutionalised. For instance, I often hear people talk in terms of 'kingdom business' or 'kingdom solicitors'. While it is true to say that a kingdom vision will inevitably lead individuals to express their calling outside the church in every sphere of life, I would see kingdom-influenced business deals and legal practices or precedents more as 'fruit of the kingdom', which in its essence is the dynamic 'kinging it' of God by the Holy Spirit. In other words, no Holy Spirit activity, no kingdom of God! The presence of the kingdom in local territory relies on the ongoing activity of the Holy Spirit. Scripture reveals to us that he prefers to work in his living temples, both personal and corporate. The church is the key agent for the kingdom.

Divine intervention

When we survey the New Testament teaching on the kingdom we cannot avoid encountering the 'already, not yet' syndrome.

On the one hand, Jesus taught that the kingdom of heaven is among or within us as believers (Lk 17:21). There is a sense that it has arrived. As he preached the gospel of the kingdom, he also demonstrated its rule by healing the sick and casting out demons (Mt 4:23–25). Furthermore, some of Jesus' parables like that of the sower, the mustard seed, the yeast, the hidden treasure and the pearl (Mt 13) clearly teach on aspects of God's kingdom that are tasted now.

On the other hand, however, Scripture clearly anticipates a future when the kingdoms of this world will become the kingdom of our Lord and of his Christ (Rev 11:15), and prophesies the consummation of the ages when all death, sickness and suffering will have been completely eradicated. Upon Jesus' return in glory, the kingdom will have arrived in fullness and totality (Rev 21). Only this cataclysmic event can finally inaugurate the kingdom in all its fullness. Some of Jesus' other parables like that of the harvest and the net clearly anticipate this time of consummation and final judgement.

In the meantime, the kingdom is "already, but not yet", and as George Eldon Ladd put it, "We live in the presence of the future." God's rule and reign can be tasted, lived in, experienced and demonstrated by the advancing church. We are exhorted not just vainly to seek first the kingdom or to keep "your kingdom come" (Mt 6:10) as a clear emphasis within our prayer life, but promised that his magnificent kingdom is near (Lk 10:9), at hand, or "within reach".[2] As the church reaches out on the tiptoes of faith to preach the good news and stand for righteousness and justice, the kingdom will 'event' through us. What is more, short of the final consummation, we are left with a challenge to pull as much of the rule and reign of God as possible into this time-space world. By God's grace, as the worldwide church moves strongly towards the Great Commission, it could be said that "we ain't seen nothing yet"!

Kingdom churches realise that Jesus-style spirituality is about seeking, going, advancing and doing. "The kingdom of heaven has been forcefully advancing, and forceful men [and women] lay hold of it" (Mt 11:12). In humility before God, our emphasis will be active and outward rather than the passive spirituality often reflected in some aspects of Christianity and the Eastern religions. Kingdom churches are not fatalistic. Rather, they realise that God's kingdom is to be apprehended and that any significant progress will almost definitely be contested by the enemy. Spiritual warfare, and the clash of the kingdom of darkness with God's kingdom, becomes a way of life for the New Testament style church.

Eschatology and evangelism

Over recent years I have come to realise just how important a healthy perspective on eschatology is. Not that we necessarily need to have a supposedly cast-iron system around which we interpret end time events. I do not propose to solve here what theologians have been debating for centuries! However, we do need to have an understanding that keeps our focus on the church's primary aim: the Great Commission. In fact, I believe that looking forward to the end of the ages and the return of Jesus is one of our primary motivations in church planting and evangelism.

A perspective that is too dominated by the present can rob people of the opportunity to live in God's hope and anticipate the glories of heaven. The gospel is stripped of its eternal dimension. However, an emphasis that sees everything as future is equally as dangerous. The church begins to dwell in remnant-itus, retreating from God's world and leaving it to rot while awaiting a divine ejector-seat (rapture). In the meantime, God awaits the generation that will preach his gospel of the kingdom "in the whole world as a testimony to all nations, and then the end will come" (Mt 24:14).

The kind of churches that need to be planted are those that realise that somehow their proclamation of the gospel to every nation, tribe, language, culture and people group is linked to the secret timing of the day and hour when Jesus will return (Mt 24:36). This is a job that needs to be done quickly and in one generation because, in the words of Gerald Coates, "Each generation is a whole new world to evangelise."

The gospel of the kingdom saves the church from a damaging 'science fiction' eschatology that is inward-looking (promoting controversy rather than God's work [1 Tim 1:4]) and motivates us 'worldward' with an excited expectation of our glorious hope in Christ. This, in my opinion, is one of the primary purposes of the New Testament passages relating to the end of the ages.

The church that has a kingdom vision will be preoccupied with God's broad purposes. Its evangelism will take on a new meaning. Life will not begin and end with our church planting or limited parochial concerns, but with the fullness of God's purposes in Christ.

> He made known to us the mystery of his will according to his good pleasure, which he purposed in Christ, to be put into effect when the times will have reached their fulfilment – to bring all things in heaven and on earth together under one head, even Christ (Eph 1:9–10).

We will be taken up with the commission that Christ has given us:

> Then Jesus came to them and said, "All authority in heaven and on earth has been given to me. Therefore go and make disciples of all nations, baptising them in the name of the

Father and of the Son and of the Holy Spirit, and teaching them to obey everything I have commanded you. And surely I will be with you always, to the very end of the age" (Mt 28:18–20).

I believe that every activity, vision, goal or foundation that we have as churches (and individuals) needs to be re-evaluated in the light of these purposes. Anything out of synchronisation with them needs to be scrapped or adjusted. When individuals understand that in their street evangelism, door-to-door work and so on they are flowing in line with God's great purposes for the church and all creation, it somehow puts that activity in a new light.

The kingdom church will pulsate with a heart for the world. Missionaries will not just be those who go overseas, but as kingdom people the church is a mission body. Each member will be called, sent, trained and released to fulfil their destiny, be it in their Jerusalem, Judea, Samaria or the ends of the earth (Acts 1:8) – or indeed all of these!

The message of the kingdom

The kingdom church will be taken up with vibrantly expressing the essential message (*Kerygma*) of the gospel. The central truth and content of salvation, and the presentation of these to the lost will be a key focus. Everything will channel us this way – our love for Jesus, our theology, eschatology, ecclesiology or any other 'ology' for that matter. All point us outwards to seeking first God's kingdom. As George Eldon Ladd observed, "The basic demand of the kingdom is a response of man's will."[3] It is our responsibility to ensure that every human being has as many opportunities to choose for Jesus as possible. Kingdom people are a people of proclamation (Rom 10:13–15; Acts 28:31).

Much time could be spent here analysing the kernel of the gospel message. Evangelicals historically have been very keen in this area. In my limited space here, however, I want to focus on how a kingdom perspective of the gospel broadens and liberates our understanding, giving us many insights which challenge some of the more traditional and established approaches to evangelism.

The kingdom is good news

The very word 'gospel' means 'good news'. Jesus-style evangelism certainly fitted that description. Good news to the poor, freedom for prisoners, sight for the blind, release for the oppressed and a proclamation of the year of the Lord's favour (Lk 4:17–19, my adaptation). Not a bad manifesto! Jesus demonstrated this in his lifestyle (Jn 2:1–11; Mt 11:18–19) which was an approach that the religious people found hard to cope with. His message was positive: it was life and good news. In this way Jesus drew people to the love, fatherhood and acceptance of God. He was not legalistic, fear-inducing or judgement orientated. In fact Jesus' harsh words were mainly reserved for the 'religious' rather than the average pagan.

Kingdom churches will be 'good newsing it' at every level, bringing life, goodness and wholeness into our communities. Our gospel content will focus on wooing people to God's grace. Aggressive and militant sandwich-board fire and brimstone is not a style Jesus employed. Perspectives on hell and judgement will be given with tears and compassion while pleading with people to taste the forgiveness, love and goodness of a heavenly Father.

This applies also to the prophetic ministry of the kingdom church which will follow more of the Jesus pattern of good news as opposed to the John the Baptist wilderness model. There was none greater than John under the Old Covenant, yet the advent of the kingdom and the New Covenant brings with it a new order of ministry. Jesus is our model as Prophet, Priest and King (Mt 11:19).

The good news of the kingdom will meet with opposition from Satan and the religious, but will be heard and received with joy by many 'tax collectors', 'sinners' and common people who realise their need (Mt 21:31). These are, after all, the people for whom the gospel was intended (Mk 2:17).

Kingdom power

The Gospels and the Acts are full of dynamic demonstrations of God's healing and delivering power. For instance, the Gospel of Matthew alone reports incidents of this type in chapters 8, 9, 10, 14, 15, 17 and 20. Proportionally, stories and teaching relating to the supernatural form a sizeable part of the overall content. As Jesus and his disciples proclaimed the rule and reign of God, the Holy Spirit confirmed and followed that proclamation with signs and wonders. Indeed, when Jesus commissioned and sent out the seventy-two in Luke 10 his instructions to them were, "Heal the sick who are there and tell them, 'The kingdom of God is near you'" (v 9): a model of proclamation that we see repeated regularly in the Book of Acts. In fact, it seems that many of the key churches there were planted out of prolific breakthroughs in evangelism often preceded by or characterised by signs and wonders (eg Jerusalem: Acts 3:1–10, 5:12–16; Iconium, Lystra, Derbe: Acts 14; Ephesus: Acts 19).

Kingdom proclamation involves sent disciples who have been trained and anointed by God to pray for the sick and deal with the demonic. The ministry of healing is not primarily, I believe, for use in the church, and it should be a key element within our evangelistic activities.

For some while now in our church we have been regularly praying for the sick in the context of our streetwork, door-to-door visitation and meetings. Time after time a word of knowledge, healing, deliverance or even a prophetic word has unlocked people's lives and situations to God and gained ground that may otherwise never have been taken.

Church-planting teams consisting of people who are filled with the power of the Holy Spirit will reproduce kingdom churches. Often these new communities can emerge very quickly when God's kingdom power begins to break out through them.

Kingdom righteousness

One of Jesus' key exhortations to his disciples was for them to "seek first his kingdom and his righteousness" (Mt 6:33). I believe that the main application here is not just the positional righteousness that comes to the believer upon salvation (2 Cor 5:21). Rather, this refers to the deep hunger which every believer should have to grow in holiness and reflect the morality and integrity of the King we proclaim.

Matthew 5–7 includes the Beatitudes and Jesus' key teaching on relational purity, righteousness and ethics. In our evangelism we must not be afraid to offer a clear and reasoned apologetic for Christian morality and ethics. Our proclamation can therefore focus on issues wider than the four spiritual laws! For instance, I heard of one polytechnic Christian Union which built relationships with the radical gay elements within the polytechnic. It then invited these people to a debate entitled 'Does Christianity have anything to offer the gay/lesbian person?'. They handled the time sensitively and clearly. As a result, their communication of Christian ethics opened up to the gospel people who would have been hardened to more classical approaches.

However, our reflection of the righteousness of God should not only be in what we say but also in who we are. Churches which plant and extend God's kingdom successfully will be those which have the moral character of the kingdom etched deeply into their relationships and personalities. By God's grace, they will be known by all (even the unbelievers) for their integrity, servanthood and for the quality of their lives.

True New Testament evangelism therefore occurs in a team context. Embryonic churches, local bodies and apostolic teams embody the gospel while proclaiming it.[4] It is by the fruit of character and the love within the team that people will discern the genuineness of our faith (Mt 7:16; Jn 13:34–35).

In the context of the team there can be accountability and an environment within which ongoing development of life, understanding and character can occur. Without this kind of evangelistic/church context sadly what many individuals build with their gift will be destroyed by their character. The age of the independent maverick evangelist is over (did it ever arrive?). All the commitment, skill, power and knowledge in and of themselves will not produce the on-going impact needed to see our communities fully networked with the gospel. The church seeking the righteousness of the kingdom will ensure that where it has attained visibility it has also developed its credibility.

Kingdom justice

Another key theme which will be a major thrust within our church life is that of justice. In Luke 4:17–22 Jesus claimed to be Messiah and announced a little of the substance of his mission:

> The scroll of the prophet Isaiah was handed to him. Unrolling it, he found the place where it is written: "The Spirit of the Lord is on me, because he has anointed me to preach good news to the poor. He has sent me to proclaim freedom for the prisoners and recovery of sight for the blind, to release the oppressed, to proclaim the year of the Lord's favour." Then he rolled up the scroll, gave it back to the attendant and sat down. The eyes of everyone in the synagogue were fastened on him, and he said to them, "Today this scripture is fulfilled in your hearing."

In this passage Jesus uses the words 'preach' (*euangelizo*) once, 'proclaim' (*kerusso*) twice and 'release' (*aphesis*) once. The word 'preach' carries the sense of declaring good news, while 'proclaim' means to herald or to announce. The word 'release' means to release from bondage, imprisonment; a release from captivity.

In the light of these broad terms and the New Testament evidence which points both ways, my approach to this passage is not completely to 'spiritualise' it, neither is it to view the passage in purely physical terms. It is clear that the gospel was preached both to the poor in spirit and to those literally poor. It releases those who are in spiritual prisons while also bringing justice to those physically detained. Both the spiritually and physically blind and oppressed are made whole. In this vein the parable of the Good Samaritan (Lk 10:29–37) and Jesus' decision to reveal his identity first to a Samaritan who was also a woman (Jn 4:1–26) are very interesting. There are many lessons that can be drawn. However, in the light of Jewish prejudices against both Samaritans and women one thing is for sure: these verses need to be seen as radical anti-racist and anti-sexist statements.

Dovetail this with the continual cry of the old Testament prophets for justice for the poor and oppressed (eg Is 1:17) and we begin to see that the very essence of the kingdom gospel is that of justice. Observing this of Christianity, one leading Muslim spokesman declared: "Human rights are a Judeo-Christian aberration!"[5]

An understanding of the kingdom gospel will release the church from a narrow, irrelevant 'piety' to become agents for change and justice in our society. Jesus called us "salt and light" (Mt 5:13–16). Salt is a preservative, a flavouring and a purifying agent. Light dispels darkness, gives direction and speaks of hope, vision and holiness.

To the kingdom thinker there is no dichotomy, tension or incompatibility between evangelism and social action. They are not mutually exclusive but are complementary, and a church living a kingdom gospel will never quite be able to work out which it is doing because all of its activities will aim to bring people to faith in Christ and improve their lives at every level.

Where do people look for justice or a body of people who will speak with one voice as advocates for the oppressed? I hope it will be to our churches – both the ones we have now and those yet to be planted.

Kingdom reconciliation

Paul observes that the church has the ministry of reconciliation (2 Cor 5:17–21). These are amazing words, that God has chosen us to represent him as ambassadors and that somehow he is making his appeal to humanity through us, his people. An exciting and incredibly humbling statement, this reconciliation ministry involves helping people to find a restored relationship with God through Jesus Christ.

However, elsewhere in the New Testament Paul reveals how completely Christ's work on the cross has brought about reconciliation. This great work involves all things: "For God was pleased to have all his fulness dwell in him, and through him to reconcile to himself all things, whether things on earth or things in heaven, by making peace through his blood, shed on the cross" (Col 1:19–20). A reconciliation of man to God, man to man (Eph 2:11–22; Gal 3:28) and also within creation (Rom 8:19–21).

Wherever the gospel of the kingdom is preached people will be falling in love with Father God, marriages will be mended, family rifts restored and forgiveness shed abroad. Hatred, prejudice and division based on race, sex or class are dispelled as God's reign and rule is experienced. Throughout the New Testament we see many examples of this occurring (eg Zacchaeus, Lk 19:1–10 or Cornelius, Acts 10:34–35).

One issue that is particularly relevant for the church to address in this manner is the issue of environmentalism. While we know that perfection and the new heaven and earth can only come finally through the return of Jesus, it is clear that the "renewal of all things" (Mt 19:28) is God's plan.

In anticipation of this, because we are stewards of creation we need to be exploring and expounding fully the Christian worldview as it relates to creation, green issues and theology (Gen 1:28; 2:15). As we do so we will find that the kingdom gospel is greener than we think!

Kingdom churches will be communities of reconciliation. Their life, outreach and history will be littered with stories of reconciliation and restoration.

The church and the kingdom

Howard Snyder observes:

> The Church gets into trouble whenever it thinks it is in the church business rather than the Kingdom business. In the church business people are concerned with church activities, religious behaviour and spiritual things. In the

Kingdom business, people are concerned with Kingdom activities, all human behaviour and everything that God has made, visible and invisible. Church people think about how to get people into the church, Kingdom people think about how to get the church into the world. Church people worry that the world might change the church, Kingdom people work to see the church change the world![16]

A kingdom understanding keeps the focus of the church where God's heart is – loving the world (Jn 3:16). It also radically transforms our perspectives on our call and vision as churches and individuals. Our vocation is no longer seen within the constrictive parameters of a secular/Christian context. As Gerald Coates observes, the only truly secular thing is sin! By contrast, we see that our calling is to every sphere of society, the world and its culture. Individual ministry therefore has a wider context than just the church sphere. Kingdom revivals will see called and anointed individuals demonstrating God's glory in every sphere of business, politics, art, music: in fact all of culture. The church witnessing fully to the kingdom will leave no stone unturned and the people in its locality will be unable to avoid a confrontation with the reign of God. Whether in the streets, at doors, in the community, social services, local politics, art, commerce or sport – all these will be full of believers being salt and light and reflecting Jesus in all they do.

Just as it is true to say that the influence of the kingdom is broader than the church, it is also true to reflect that the kingdom comes through the church's ministry. The church is the instrument of the kingdom and the custodian of it. The kingdom comes through the ministry of the church, the body to whom Jesus has given its keys (Mt 16:19; 18:18). There is a sense in which the church opens the kingdom to some and closes it to others. As the messenger and message are received, the blessings of the kingdom are imparted, but as they are rejected so too is God himself (Lk 10:8–10,16).

So the kingdom of God created the church. As H D Wendland writes: "The Church is but the result of the coming of God's Kingdom into the world by the mission of Jesus Christ."[7]

Yet the church is not the kingdom. As Martin Scott points out, "The Kingdom of God is primarily the dynamic rule and reign of God and secondarily the sphere in which this rule is experienced. The Church is the community of the Kingdom but never the Kingdom itself. The Church is the people of the Kingdom but never the Kingdom itself."

Or, in the words of George Eldon Ladd, "The Kingdom is the rule of God, the Church is the society of men."

A kingdom lens brings the fullness of God's purpose into focus. It is perhaps the major ingredient in church growth. With the kingdom in mind we will be preserved from a lopsided gospel or one that is privatised; bound up within so-called sacred territory and irrelevant to the normal person. In it we find the true meaning of discipleship in any age.

The gospel of the kingdom is three-dimensional: words (our proclamation), works (righteousness, justice, reconciliation), and wonders (the supernatural) (Rom 15:17–20). Like Paul our aim should be to see this gospel "fully proclaimed" throughout the whole earth.

Notes

1. Martin Scott, "The Kingdom of God", *Equipped to Lead*, 1991.
2. Roger Forster, "The Kingdom of God", *Together for the Kingdom*, Pioneer Tapes.
3. George Eldon Ladd, *Gospel of the Kingdom*.
4. *Vines Dictionary of New Testament Words*.
5. Article in *Independent* newspaper
6. Howard Snyder, *Liberating the Church*.
7. Martin Scott, "The Kingdom of God", *Equipped to Lead*. Quoting from H D Wendland, *The Kingdom of God and History*.

Chapter 3

Discipleship

We have looked at how Jesus gathered his disciples, and have examined, in brief, a little of the type of gospel that needs to be embodied and proclaimed by the advancing and growing church. We are now going to look at the whole issue of discipleship.

Planting and church growth at the level we need will not be achieved by a church adhering to a professional or elitist approach to ministry and serving God. The concept of clergy and laity (priest and congregation) will need to be discarded from our thinking if we are to move forward. Sadly, even churches which give lip service to the priesthood of all believers (1 Pet 2:9–12) still live a strange contradiction in their lives. Women are excluded from leadership and ministry and in real terms their pastor or leading elder is just a vicar by another name who wears a different outfit! Our view of the process of discipleship needs to be reformed, moving away from our personal and private development into a good and reliable church member, towards a life of usefulness to God – serving him and seeking first the kingdom. Every church member needs to appreciate their call and realise that there are no limits to how that can be pursued within the context of our churches. Ministry is not just for an elite few so-called full timers.

A community of disciples and a discipling community.

As Christians we have all been individually called (Rom 1:6) and God has prepared good works for us to do in advance of our rising to the challenge of this calling (Eph 2:10). Every believer is gifted, has the gift of the Holy Spirit and can be used both supernaturally and otherwise in God's service. It is what we are here for!

However, the church is also corporately called. Individually we are but disembodied limbs; together we are the body of Christ (1 Cor 12:12–31). Individually we are temples of the Holy Spirit (1 Cor 6:19), but corporately we are a more powerful and glorious temple which has a greater destiny (Eph 2:11–22).

The church should be a body within which people are educated and motivated both for and by God's purposes. Our corporate power and impact is greater than the sum total of the individual parts if we were left to our own devices. We need to become communities that are dynamic, motivating, redeeming, commissioning and sending.

When people are born again into this kind of environment, a sense of calling and a desire to be radically discipled will often be an integral part of their conversion experience. I remember a situation with a couple who are now key members of one of our church plants. I had grown up with the man but we had not seen each other for quite some time. When we met again he was living with a girl, but they were both very open to the gospel. Many discussions were had around virtually every apologetic issue. They loved a debate. The historicity of Jesus, the reliability of the Scriptures, the possibility of the miraculous, right through to Christianity versus Marxism were all debated at length. In the midst of this I was best man at their wedding! Sometime later the girl came to an evangelistic meeting while her husband was on an Open University course. She was duly converted and a week later I prophesied a simple and apparently insignificant word to her.

She rushed home, recounted the prophetic word, and as she did so her husband was overcome by the Holy Spirit feeling a sensation like waves rushing over him! They prayed together and he was then converted. At this stage I was called in to make sure that he had properly given his life to the Lord. Before I had a chance to present a *Journey Into Life* he exclaimed, "I've given my whole life to Jesus, received his forgiveness and he's called me to serve him with all my creative abilities." At that stage I discarded the *Journey Into Life*. For Mark, his calling was a fundamental part of his conversion, and so it should be. With this foundation every member of our communities will be keen to be changed, developed and taught. Rather than missionaries being seen merely as those who are sent out overseas we will realise that the church is a mission body and we are all missionaries.

Jesus called us to "go" (Mt 28:19) and therefore all Christians are "goers". All of us will be going somewhere. In the immediate this may mean a foundation course, leadership training, being part of an evangelistic team, leading worship, serving practically or travelling overseas. All will have a focus and will receive the relevant encouragement and development in accordance with their personal situation.

A disciple is a learner, being transformed, sanctified empowered and equipped. No matter how long we've been Christians we will always be disciples (learners) and so will always be learning and changing. One of the characteristics of Christian maturity is therefore constant change. The fact is that God wants putty, not well-taught, spiritually gifted rocks!

Jesus and Paul

Jesus' disciples followed him (Mt 4:18–20) and travelled with him learning (being taught) in both public and private forums (Mt 13:1–9). He gave them opportunities (Lk 10:1–16), and taught them how to cope with success and how to learn amid failure (Mk 9:14–29). He dealt with their attitudes and character (Mt 20:20–28), their basic motivation and allowed them to experience truth first hand for themselves (Mt 16:16–17). He dealt with them firmly when they needed it (Mt 16:22–23). He nurtured them, cared for them, prayed for them (Lk 22:31–32), and his investment saw them though the traumas of his death into the joy of his resurrection and their empowering at Pentecost.

The Apostle Paul seemed to follow a similar model with his trainees. He cared for them in a fatherly manner (2 Tim 1:2), and they travelled with him experiencing on-the-job training. Alongside this, it is clear that he imparted gifting and ministry to them through training, and the laying-on of hands (Tit 1:5, 2 Tim 1:6–7). This is the kind of discipling that equips people for service, leadership and usefulness rather than inactivity and a self-indulgent faith. People's gifts and talents are harnessed for God's kingdom and not just left to be squandered in ways that do not advance the broad purposes of God. Surely this discipleship is for all Christians and not a chosen minority of activists?

Of course, these New Testament models of discipleship have historical roots in both Judaism and the Old Testament (eg prophetic schools, 2 Kings 2:15) which we have no space to explore here. However, it should be noted that these models differ considerably from much of the Greek style, knowledge-based systems that prevail in much of Christian discipleship today. I believe that if we could only learn some basic lessons from this on-the-job lifestyle training then our church life could be considerably enhanced. In any case, the church is the ideal environment for this kind of training as it is able on an ongoing basis to facilitate both the more theoretical and practical aspects of development.

So much of the training Jesus gave his disciples was earthed in relationship, friendship and sharing as they ate, drank and lived together. The church ideally should be made up of relationships, friendships and community – the perfect environment for Jesus-style discipleship.

Friendship is never meant to be self-indulgent, but is supposed to be inclusive of others, promoting growth, maturity, training and development in the church (Eph 4:15–16). Exhortation, rebuke, encouragement and comfort are the substance of church life and the means by which growth is secured and real, honest relationships established.

Fellowship that is actually going somewhere is friendship which is mutually resourcing, shaping one another for service and provoking one another to good works that advance God's kingdom.

Characteristics of the disciple

During the ferment of discipleship in a growing church it is essential at all times to keep our focus on character and be careful with our natural attraction to gifting. We are in a society which minimalises the need for integrity, stability and character, and exalts people who are dynamically gifted, even though they may be emotionally insecure and inadequate. Often the results of this are disastrous. So many movie stars, sports personalities and politicians fit this bill that I'll avoid personal illustrations and the resulting libel suits!

Often in the church an apparent lack of gifted people of stable character causes us to seize unhelpfully on immature but gifted people and give them profile beyond their ability to cope at that stage. It is true that risks need to be taken. People need to be given room and if we wait for perfection then we'll have very little emerging ministry. I often look back with amusement at what I was like when I first began to be used by God – something of which on occasions my wife also gleefully reminds me!

Nevertheless, our discipleship needs to have a primary focus on character, and people need to know that while their gifting is being shaped the major qualification for leadership and usefulness is a developing character. In fact, in Paul's list of qualifications for overseers (1 Tim 3:1–13) only one gifting is mentioned and that lies in the area of teaching. All others lie in the area of character.

Humility and vulnerability

In Matthew 18:1-6 Jesus identifies a childlike attitude as one of the primary requirements for entry into the kingdom of God.

It could easily be added that without this our growth process in Christ will also be stunted. In verse 4 he particularly homes in on the characteristic of humility. Children are naturally responsive and teachable. They believe the best and have a natural openness, vulnerability and faith. This is why I have many friends who, when sick, would far rather be prayed for by their children because they seem to see better results!

If people are to grow in God two of the first qualities they need to learn are humility and vulnerability. With these they are able to open up before God and people more mature in faith, and to take the position of a learner. This attitude is endemic to the growing church.

In my experience an excited zeal will also be a normal feature in the life of any convert who has been born properly into God's kingdom. However, if this zeal is not tempered with a teachable spirit they probably will not get much further in God without the Lord teaching them some hard lessons. In fact if their zeal is really initiated by the Holy Spirit, openness and humility should be its fruit. I remember a young man who was converted some years ago and was full of zeal and enthusiasm for God. He was a person who had much raw potential. Unfortunately, within about three weeks he felt he had uncovered all the secrets of church life and set about causing pastoral havoc and lecturing the leaders with some heretical theology. His pride was clearly a cover up for a deep insecurity but he was unable to face this and despite all the care and patience of many in the church, he has now faded into obscurity. I sense that he will continue to be lost to God's purposes until he learns this crucial lesson.

Humility is not a characteristic often exalted and admired in Western culture. Strength, self-sufficiency and independence are often seen as desirable. However, God's kingdom is the antithesis of this; indeed God opposes the proud but gives grace to the humble (1 Pet 5:5). When looking for people to invest their lives in, leaders would do well to select the most teachable and humble.

People who have this attitude will be able to cope with the inevitable consequences of Jesus-style discipleship. Alongside all the joys, privileges and excitement (Lk 10:17), there are times of failure (Mk 9:17), the exposure of our Godless motives (Mt 20:26) as well as our insecurities and fears. Often the most fruitful times of growth are not in the teaching session but are in the midst of sharing our deep secrets and fears with those who believe in us and will minister God's love, healing, acceptance and some wise advice.

In my limited experience, the young Christians who grow quickest into stable leadership are those who are open. In our church there are many who have been trusted with important areas of responsibility at least in part due to their openness. Because you know where you are with them, you know you can trust them.

An example of this would be one of our men who took me to one side explaining that in all the busy routine of life and ministry there had been pressure in his marriage. Tiredness had reduced the regularity of their sex life, small arguments had resulted and he had found himself having to work to control his thoughts. I was overjoyed at his openness and that he cared more about his integrity than about his obvious giftedness and giving a 'flawless performance' to his leader.

Once the problem was shared its power was broken. A little advice, prayer and some diary adjustments and his marriage had very soon recaptured its original joy and excitement. I left knowing that here was a man I could trust, not because of his perfection, but because of his openness. Only this kind of discipleship will produce the quality required within our churches. If our leadership is insecure and papers over the cracks, avoiding confrontation and the more sensitive issues, our people will experience lopsided growth. They will be full of Bible knowledge and theory which has not been grounded in their everyday life and experience.

Servanthood and faithfulness

Another fundamental characteristic is servanthood. This is another quality not often exalted in the context of society at large. Success is seen in terms of status and having others serve you rather than being a servant. The pyramid system is seen as an ideal model in business, and sadly much church leadership training tries to adopt these principles. While I am sure there are things that can be learned from business, as John Noble once said, "As far as I'm concerned all the pyramids are in Egypt.". Much business-style leadership is based on a power-and-status worldly model and is therefore incompatible with church life.

Jesus said:

> You know that the rulers of the Gentiles lord it over them, and their high officials exercise authority over them. Not so with you. Instead, whoever wants to become great among you must be your servant, and whoever wants to be first must be your slave – just as the Son of Man did not come to be served, but to serve, and to give his life as a ransom for many (Mt 20:25–28).

People's vision needs to be orientated into the life of Jesus. It is clear that he saw spiritual stature in terms of servanthood and sacrificial lifestyle rather than status. For many, their natural instincts lead them to draw significance and acceptance from having a position or function in the church. In fact some people find it difficult to operate unless first given a position. Sadly many ecclesiastical structures support this kind of attitude. If we pamper to this mentality we will ultimately grieve the Holy Spirit. As an antidote, we need to profile opportunities to serve rather than status and position. It is as people begin to enjoy the privilege of serving that they begin to grow and develop. Every believer should have this desire to move forward out of their love for Jesus and not because there is a 'carrot' of church responsibility before their eyes!

Flowing from this, Jesus taught another key principle which must be a fundamental part of our discipleship within church. That is being "faithful with a few things" (Mt 25:21). In the context of the parable of the talents there are many things to be learned, but one key is certainly the fact that proving faithful with small areas of gifting and responsibility is the gateway and process through which the Lord releases us into a wider sphere. Therefore, irrespective of the person's age, natural abilities or secular qualifications, I feel that it is foolish to release people into any responsibility until they have proved faithful in the little.

The whole process of testing and proving is obviously a key part of selection for local church leadership (1 Tim 3:10), but it should also be an aspect of every area of discipleship within the church. If people cannot first be relied upon to turn up on time to put a few chairs out for the meeting, it is unlikely that they will make reliable assistant house-group leaders. As people are taught this they will eagerly give themselves to the Lord knowing that he who exalts himself the Lord humbles and vice versa (Lk 18:14). If you try to hold on to your life you will lose it. However, if you give it up for the sake of the kingdom you will surely find it (Mt 10:39).

With this kind of heart any Christian will be receiving all kinds of spiritual gifts and equipping from the Lord and will also be in the right position to have their natural abilities shaped and harnessed for God's kingdom.

Qualities of the disciple

The desire to be used by God and to serve others needs to be at epidemic proportions in our churches. The environment of sharing with and ministering to one another should be so evident that new converts very soon become involved, under supervision, in discipling others. With this happening people learn quickly. A while back my wife and I were speaking at a large youth training event attended by a group of our teenagers who were mainly new converts. We were both tired and my wife particularly felt drained and under pressure. During the worship one evening one of our young Christians whom my wife had discipled observed this, approached her, offered 'textbook' counsel and prayed with authority into her life. It was a great joy for me to see her learning these things and also that she felt free to practise on us!

In real terms, then, every Christian should be looking to give away that which God has already given them, whether they have been a Christian for six months or six years. Alongside this the church needs to develop a cell or house group-type system, not merely for pastoral maintenance, but to enable and train leadership to gather people together to be trained, taught and shaped. I will look at this process in more detail when we consider the training of leaders in a later chapter.

These key leaders need to have been proved and tested, being able to operate as examples (1 Pet 5:3). While keeping a focus on the perfection of Jesus, these need to be people who can confidently say, "Follow my example, as I follow the example of Christ" (1 Cor 11:1). People need to see the way forward encapsulated by their leadership who are not the kind of shepherds who drive the flock from behind but who lead gently, by example, from the front. As Gerald Coates observes, leadership requires a degree of moral superiority. Dudley Daniels points out: "If leaders are not one step ahead of the flock, the church will have to backslide in order to get behind them!" In a similar vein Paul had no hesitation in writing this to the Philippians:

> Finally, brothers, whatever is true, whatever is noble, whatever is right, whatever is pure, whatever is lovely, whatever is admirable – if anything is excellent or praiseworthy – think about such things. Whatever you have learned or received or heard from me, or seen in me – put it into practice. And the God of peace will be with you (Phil 4:8–9).

Our example as leaders will only have effect if it flows from an accessibility of life and ongoing relationship with our people. Leaders who act like civil dignitaries, keeping themselves one step removed from the people, or who are afraid or unable to make friends, will only find limited success. This is because relationship provides the only context for real ongoing discipleship. The examples of Jesus with his disciples and Paul with his teams further support this. These relationships will not all operate at the same level. For some it will be a peer level friendship, while for others it may be an elder brother/sister (1 Tim 5:1–2) or even a parenting type relationship (2 Tim 1:2). In all of this the relationship skills of the discipler are of paramount importance. The ability to open your heart and life, to gain people's trust and to draw the best out of them is of paramount importance. If people feel secure and cared for; that you are available to them at all times and that you genuinely want to help them in any way possible, then the doors will open for development to occur. Appropriate instruction can be given and this can be earthed at an individual level during more intimate times of sharing, prayer and study.

In our church we like to encourage an expectation and desire within the congregation to be shaped and developed. We try to make the most of every opportunity. For instance, we encourage our house-group leaders to prepare their group members to begin to contribute publicly in our meetings. After they have done so it is generally understood that some form of feedback will be given to encourage and help the person to improve further.

For instance, often an item shared publicly, be it teaching or a prophetic word, may lack a little in terms of biblical content, illustration or style. I remember one occasion when one of our house-group leaders (who has since become a leader within one of our church plants) stood up to share some teaching. The content, illustrations and delivery were good except for the way she was continually and nervously shuffling her feet as she stood. As a result nobody heard the teaching. We were all transfixed by her training shoes! After the meeting I encouraged her and then later in the week took the opportunity to give my observations in full. She received them gracefully and has continued to grow in God.

The church must be a safe environment in which people feel free to make mistakes and step out without losing credibility. They can do this if they feel their leaders are looking on and will dig them out of any holes if necessary! The person who becomes defensive and is reluctant to receive such input needs patient care until he has come to the place of openness and humility before God where he is more open to taking the learning role of a disciple.

Alongside this we need to take every opportunity possible to expose people to new experiences of God. In all but the most sensitive situations we encourage our leaders wherever possible to counsel someone alongside a less experienced person. A process of mentoring then begins to take place and people learn on the job. Similarly, we encourage more mature people in the church to open their marriages, lives and lifestyles to others. For example, the opportunity for newly-weds to see how mature couples relate (warts and all!),what their pressure points are and how, for instance, they operate financially, again helps them to grow in character. They see how other couples have earthed biblical concepts in real-life situations.

The gospel of the kingdom gives us a broad sphere of operation as church. This means there are many areas of service people can give themselves to in order to learn fresh things in God. Locally we have teams working regularly in evangelism, on different social action projects, in management and resources, youth work and childrens work. All of these teams plug into our churchwide leadership training as well as having training modules of their own. Broad exposure to these gives people ample opportunity to touch the heart of God and discover their calling and ministry.

All of this takes much time and a good deal of resources. I remember one year when I only spoke six times in the church because I was observing others whom I had trained. In the short term, delegation takes more work, can be more frustrating and requires a commitment from leaders who are willing to give time in the development of others rather than filling the pulpit every week. As we as leaders begin to fit the jigsaw pieces together we will find ourselves reproducing over and over again the ministries needed to facilitate regular church planting.

Chapter 4

Spiritual Warfare

Whole areas of the world are under the power of Satan and his fallen angels. In fact the Scriptures make it clear that 'the whole world lies in the power of the evil one' (1 Jn 5:19). How has this come about?

To begin with, Satan and his troops had legitimate authority over the earth and its territory with the rest of the angels for the outworking of the purposes of God. Jesus clearly identifies Satan as prince or ruler of this world, and the writer to the Hebrews describes the original purpose of all angels: 'Are they not all ministering spirits, sent out to render service for the sake of those who will inherit salvation?' (Heb 1:14). Secondly, Satan broke faith with God and his stewardship and began to set up his own anti-kingdom by tempting and subverting the human race. In so doing, he found the way to grip and bind individual persons in order to keep them under his lordship. Thirdly, he used these individual humans to pursue his own negative spiritual desires in the world and set up strongholds of sinful activity which he could inhabit and so subvert his and their proper role in the earth, substituting instead his own anti-kingdom and wickedness.

If we are to be successful church planters, planting churches that plant churches, then this satanic power has to be attacked and broken, and strongholds of heaven set up in its place. Failure in this realm explains at least in part the failure of preceding generations to get the gospel into the whole earth and see Jesus return in fulfilment of the Great Commission.

Breaking Satan's power is achieved on these three levels: by gaining ground in those heavenly, spiritual spheres of the earth currently inhabited by Satan; by casting out demons; and by breaking strongholds of satanic power in society and substituting the church and its kingdom influence instead.

In this chapter we will seek to clarify the biblical grounds for these perspectives, and to provide practical guidance for spiritual warfare in the church-planting context. We will look first at principalities and powers and how to deal with them, then demonisation in individuals and how to break it, and finally at satanic strongholds in society and how to shift them.

Principalities and powers and how to deal with them

The Scriptures make it clear that Satan is the spiritual prince of this world; that he is the prince of the other demons; that they are spirit beings like angels; and that he is the subversive leader of an anti-kingdom opposed to God and his purposes.

Satan is prince of this world

Jesus describes Satan in these terms on three separate occasions recorded by John. When foretelling his death he says, 'Now is the time for judgment on this world; now the prince of this world will be driven out' (Jn 12:31, NIV) Again, as he approaches the cross, he says, '... the prince of this world is coming. He has no hold on me' (Jn 14:30, NIV). He says that the coming Holy Spirit will convict the world of judgement 'because the prince of this world now stands condemned' (Jn 16:11, NIV) In each case the Greek word used by the Lord Jesus is 'archon', a ruler or chief, and is the singular form of the word for principalities used by Paul writing to the Ephesians. Paul speaks of 'the prince of the power of the air, of the spirit that is now working in the sons of disobedience' (Eph 2:2). He says, 'We are not contending against flesh and blood, but against the principalities, against the powers, against the world rulers of this present darkness, against the spiritual hosts of wickedness in the heavenly places' (Eph 6:12).

Now the use of this terminology by Jesus and its expansion by Paul clearly implies both right and territory belonging to the devil; right which he has abused and territory which he has wrongly stewarded, but right and territory nonetheless. This makes sense of a number of important, but at first sight difficult, passages of Scripture such as Satan's claim that the kingdoms of the world had been given to him (Lk 4:6), his presence in the councils of heaven (Job 1:6) and indeed his presence in the garden at the beginning of creation (Gen 3:1). These were his rightful positions and places. What was wrong was what he had done with his positions and power.

Satan is prince of demons

When the 72 returned from their mission with the delighted news that even the demons were subject to them in Jesus' name, Jesus specifically identified the demons with Satan (Lk 10:14-19). Again, when the Pharisees accused him of casting out demons by Beelzebub the prince of demons, he rejected their allegation but not the concept of Satan ruling over lesser demons. He said, ' if Satan casts out Satan he is divided against himself; how then shall his kingdom stand? And if I by Beelzebub cast out demons, by whom do your sons cast them out?' (Mt 12:26–27) This is the clear implication of Paul's previously quoted statement to the Ephesians, for when he speaks of our struggle with principalities and powers it is in the context of standing firm against the devil. John in Revelation makes the position even more clear when he speaks of war in heaven, 'Michael and his angels waging war with the dragon. And the dragon and his angels waged war ... and the great dragon was thrown down, the serpent of old who is called the devil and Satan' (Rev 12:7–9). So as well as having right and territory, Satan has an organisation of demons over which he reigns.

Satan and his demons are spirit beings like angels

The nature and purpose of angels is quite clear in Scripture. The writer to the Hebrews says, 'Are they not all ministering spirits, sent out to render service for the sake of those who will inherit salvation?' (Heb 1:14). Jesus himself explicitly states that children and little ones who have been stumbled in life have angels working for them: 'See that you do not despise one of these little ones, for I say to you, that their angels in heaven continually behold the face of My Father who is in heaven' (Mt 18:10).

John writes in his Revelation of angels being attached to churches (Rev 2:1, 8, 12) and in the Old Testament they are involved with the distribution and setting up of the nations. This is the simplest way to understand how the Lord scattered the nations abroad from Babel (Gen 11:8) in such an ordered fashion that Paul could describe in Athens as 'having determined ... the boundaries of their habitation' (Acts 17:26). This is the distinct statement of Deuteronomy in the Septuagint and in the Dead Sea scrolls. 'When the Most High gave the nations their inheritance, when He separated the sons of man, He set the boundaries of the peoples according to the number of the sons of [God]' (Deut 32:8). The Masoretic text has 'the sons of Israel', but the Septuagint text that Jesus himself would have used makes the best sense, especially in the light of the territorial responsibilities of Satan which we have already noted and those of other senior angelic beings described by Daniel to which we shall refer again shortly.

In the Old Testament the phrase 'sons of God' is clearly a description of angelic beings, as in Job 1: 'Now there was a day when the sons of God came to present themselves before the Lord, Satan also came among them' (v 6). This is so obviously a reference to angels that the translators of the NIV had no hesitation in substituting 'angels' for 'sons of God' in their translation. It is a pity that they were less than consistent when they translated Deuteronomy 32!

So we can conclude that the proper sphere of angelic ministry is at least to individuals, to churches and to nations and their territories. This is underlined further still when we consider the explicit biblical teaching on the activities of Satan and the demons, who were originally angels themselves. The same word for angels in Hebrews 1 where they are described as 'spirits' is exactly the same as the word used for a demon in Luke 9. The only difference is that angels are described as 'ministering' spirits whereas the demons are 'unclean' spirits: 'the demon dashed him to the ground ... but Jesus rebuked the unclean spirit' (Lk 9:42). Satan and the demons are involved with individual people, just as angels are, but in this case it is to afflict, oppress and bind. They are involved with the people of God in both Old and New Testament expressions, but no longer to serve, instead to accuse and destroy: 'He showed me Joshua the high priest standing before the angel of the Lord, and Satan standing at his right hand to accuse him' (Zech 3:1); 'Satan ... the accuser of our brethren' (Rev 12:9–10). Satan and his demons control territory, but no longer in the hope that men will feel after God and find him, but in order to blind them to the truth and to hinder their prayers. As Paul puts it, 'The god of this world has blinded the minds of the unbelieving, that they might not see the light of the gospel of the glory of Christ' (2 Cor 4:4).

Daniel is the most explicit, next to Jesus, about the territorial aspects of Satan's power. He records for us his prayer battles and the angelic backdrop to them. In the words of his angelic visitor:

> From the first day that you set your heart on understanding this and on humbling yourself before your God, your words were heard, and I have come in response to your words. But the prince of the kingdom of Persia was withstanding me for twenty-one days; then behold, Michael, one of the chief princes, came to help me ...Do you understand why I came to you? But I shall now return to fight against the prince of Persia; so I am going forth, and behold, the prince of Greece is about to come' (Dan 10:12–13; 20).

These angelic princes are clearly differentiated from the earthly rulers such as Cyrus King of Persia mentioned at the beginning of the same chapter. The moral to all this is clear. If we are to see the restoration and return that Daniel prayed for in New Testament terms, and plant churches which network the world with the good news of the kingdom of God in our time, then we must recognise the existence of these territorial beings just as Daniel did, and discover how to engage heaven in our prayers.

Satan is the subversive leader of the anti-Christ kingdom

Jesus initiated his three years of public ministry with a Holy Spirit led, deliberate sortie into the wilderness to encounter Satan and resist him. We need to understand and follow his practice in our own church-planting strategy.

For the moment we need to observe the significance of his deliberate encounters with Satan in understanding the foundations of Satan's anti-kingdom strongholds in society. We have noted these in outline in chapter one. Now we need to recognise even more seriously the materialism, power lust and status-seeking uncovered in the temptations. The fact that these were the temptations that the prince of this world loosed against the Son of God himself implies strongly that these are the worldly, social manifestations of Satan's kingdom in all times and places. Furthermore, these will be the basic strongholds of enemy power in human society at all times, and the specific socio-cultural and historical variations of satanic power in both individuals and society at large will be rooted in them.

This has certainly proved to be the case in our experience. This is especially significant in evaluating the church-planting context of the Western world, where these anti-kingdom values form a major part of the accepted and legitimate cultural and social norms of the day. If we are going to succeed against them, as Jesus did throughout his ministry, culminating at the cross, then there is a fierce and extraordinary spiritual battle we simply have to engage in.

In our experience it is necessary to deal with these 'principalities and powers in the heavenly places' in at least three ways before we can really exercise authority over them in individuals or in the structures of society. We need to deal with their effects on ourselves personally; we need to resist and bind them by the exercise of our own personal God-given authority; and we need to take authority over them together with other members of the body of Christ with whom we corporately form a stronghold for God, increasingly attacking and displacing the power base of Satan.

Winning back personal ground from Satan

In the introductory chapter I mentioned the need for progressive discipleship; for advance on the internal frontier of the kingdom of God to match advance on the external frontier. Much of this personal discipleship growth relates to retaking ground from Satan and his principalities and powers where their influence has contaminated the territory of our own personal lives. On the cross Jesus disarmed the principalities and powers (Col 2:15). Just before, he states the secret of his power to succeed: 'The ruler of the world is coming, and he has nothing in Me' (Jn 14:30). Our task is to move increasingly towards this position of integrity. We are all part of a fallen world. We have all sinned and come short of the glory of God. But on top of this we, in the West at least, have been socialised into a society which God has had to take his hand off in judgement, and in which the influences of Satan have grown very bold and strong in consequence.

This is abundantly clear from even a cursory study of Romans 1. We have suppressed the truth (v18), dishonoured God (v21), worshipped human beings (v23) and therefore incurred God's specific judgement on our society. We have been given over to our chosen way of impurity (v24), lies (v25), immorality (v26), depravity (v28) and death (v32). We have to get this judgement off our backs! The good news is that we can (v16). But not only do we need to receive God's free mercy and grace in forgiveness through the cross, we need to put off 'the unfruitful deeds of darkness' (Eph 5:11) and 'be renewed in the spirit of [our] mind, and put on the new self, which in the likeness of God has been created in righteousness and holiness of the truth' (Eph 4:23-24).

These deeds of darkness are particularly the materialism, power lust and status-seeking that Satan tempted Jesus with and which are so prevalent in contemporary society. We need to be ruthless in destroying any and every basis for them in the thoughts, attitudes and actions of our personal lives. If we do not do this we will be powerless to shift these same demonic powers off individuals enslaved by them, nor will we produce strongholds of the Holy Spirit together with our fellow Christians. Instead, the seeds of our downfall and the rebuilding of Satan's kingdom will be inherent in the churches we plant through our unsanctified lives.

To be intensely practical, we must watch out for materialism with regard to our money and possessions. We should give well over the top of our tithe; share our house or flat regularly with others; let other people drive our car or borrow our bike. We must avoid the lust for power like the plague and develop an acute sensitivity to our own tendency to control or manipulate people or situations, especially when we are in a place of leadership. We must refuse the glory of status for ourselves, repudiate the narcissistic self-satisfaction of being who we are and repent the moment we begin fancying ourselves.

At the same time we need to be on guard against the flip-side of this enemy activity: the damage that causes us to react into a poverty spirit, a fear or rejection of spiritual authority and the proper structures of leadership, or a sense of worthlessness and uselessness in the company of others. As we go on embracing the ultimate worth of our Lord Jesus so we humbly discover our own ultimate worth and can get on with his great work.

Developing a personal stance of active resistance

Jesus was led by the Spirit into personal, victorious encounters with Satan through various forms of fasting and prayer, often alone in the wilderness, by the sea or on the mountains. This was where he learned to bind the strong man and plunder his house (Mt 12:29).

The areas in which we go to plant churches are populated by people who are at this present moment personally oppressed and blinded by satanic powers. We have to become and remain free from the powers ourselves if we are to penetrate the darkness in partnership with the Holy Spirit. Sometimes we have been surprised by the dreadful revelations which uncover the lives and reputations of erstwhile evangelists and church leaders. We wonder how they fell so far or so fast.

But it is precisely this dynamic of spiritual warfare that explains it all. We are attacked by the powers of darkness that we seek to shift. In fact we need to realise that we are positively taking them on by going out against them in the name of Jesus. We must not be taken by surprise. Jesus began his ministry by taking on Satan in the territory of Judea under the Holy Spirit's direction. He encountered his deceptive strongholds as personal temptations and won an initial victory with the cry of resistance:'Begone, Satan!' (Mt 4:10). But Satan only left him, the Son of God, 'until an opportune time' (Lk 4:13). We are not provided with the details of those other opportune moments, although we are frequently reminded that Jesus slipped away alone somewhere (cf Lk 4:42:, 5:16). And we have already seen that he was in the practice of binding Satan (Mt 12:29) and promised us that we could do the same (Mt 16:19; Lk 10:19). What is clear is that although Satan was looking for opportune moments, Jesus and the Holy Spirit pre-empted him by going into the wilderness 'to be tempted by the devil' (Mt 4:1).

Some people have wondered at the Lord's Prayer: '...and do not lead us into temptation, but deliver us from evil.' The point is increasingly to pre-empt Satan, not being 'led *into* temptation' but being led to encounter him and to be ready for the attack as Jesus was. He is not praying to avoid the battle but for the Father's kingdom to come. This is why the various forms of fasting and prayer that the Gospels and the rest of Scripture describe are so helpful. If we are going to prove both Peter and James right and successfully resist the devil (cf Jas 4:7; 1 Pet 5:9) then we must be ready for him. We must make a way for the Holy Spirit over the flesh in our lives, whether it be sacrificing our time or abstaining from food, various kinds of drink, sleep, or sexual experience as the Lord did, and as he leads us (cf Mt 6:16-18).

I have found it extremely helpful and strategic in my own role in church planting to make it a regular, almost daily, habit to resist the enemy on the fronts of possessions, power and status as well as the related areas of pride, covetousness, immorality, unbelief and dead religion. Of course they have not all completely shifted from the territory of my own life yet, let alone all the churches for which I have some responsibility or the territories in which we aim to plant more. But Jesus did not clear the enemy out totally at his first recorded temptations. Indeed he subsequently cast out demons and Satan many times. But he still was not cast right out. Just before the cross he said, 'Now judgment is upon this world; now the ruler of this world shall be cast out' (Jn 12:31). We know that on the cross Satan *was* cast out and the long prophesied death blow to his head was dealt (Gen 3:15).

But it is not over until it is over! And so in the Revelation it is we 'the saints', who finally overcome him, by the word of our testimony, the blood of the Lamb and by not loving our lives even unto death (cf Rev 12:10–11). So we must get on with it!

The victory of Christ is there to be appropriated by the advancing church. It is after all our rightful place as human beings in dependence on God to have authority and dominion in the earth. Satan and his powers as ministering spirits were supposed to be helping us together with the rest of the angels. While it is right to respect Satan's power and original position, we should in no way be afraid of him now.

In fact Jesus promises to give us his position if we overcome. Satan was the original Morning Star, according to Isaiah; the one whose brightness helped usher in the dawning of God's purposes for his creation. But he fell from glory. 'How you have fallen from heaven, O star of the morning, son of the dawn!' (Is 14:12). But Jesus came to take that name and position back from him. Now it is Jesus who is 'the root and the offspring of David, the bright morning star' (Rev 22:16). Jesus promises this very authority to us if we overcome in humble, dependent trust in him: 'And he who overcomes, and he who keeps My deeds until the end, to him I will give authority over the nations ... and I will give him the morning star' (Rev 2:26, 28).

Developing a heavenly stronghold together with brothers and sisters

Although, like Jesus, we need to develop our own personal prayer life in the context of which we can resist the devil, we also need to learn to work together with our Christian brothers and sisters in this battle. Even Jesus needed the support of his disciples. As we have seen, it was church that he came to initiate. So when the battle was nearing its climax in Jesus' day, he called together his disciples into the garden to pray, and he told them, 'Watch with Me' (Mt 26:38). We need to watch and pray and resist Satan together as Jesus asked the disciples to.

The Garden of Gethsemane was a place of intense battle. Satan had already entered one of the twelve. The core leadership of the embryonic church, what Paul calls 'a dwelling of God in the Spirit' (Eph 2:22), was under phenomenal attack. Jesus had already warned Peter of his own personal danger from Satan (Lk 22:31). Now he tells them, 'Keep watching and praying, that you may not come into temptation' (Mk 14:38). On that occasion they failed. As a result there was a temporary, but cosmically serious, victory for the devil. Jesus responded to his captors when they arrived, 'This is your hour and the power of darkness' (Lk 22:53, RSV). Gloriously, the Lord stood firm for us, drew Satan out and triumphed over him in the cross and resurrection. Now he has ascended to the right hand of power.

Because he has pioneered the way, it is possible for us to do what the early disciples failed to do – to watch and pray and overcome the powers of darkness in our generation. Paul tells us what to do when 'the days are evil' (Eph 5:16). We should attend to the quality of our lives, as we have been considering. But he also tells us to get together and worship in the Holy Spirit and to stand firm together against the devil:

> Stand firm against the schemes of the devil. For our struggle is not against flesh and blood, but against the rulers, against the powers, against the world forces of this darkness, against the spiritual forces of wickedness in the heavenly places ... resist in the evil day ... extinguish all the flaming missiles of the evil one (Eph 6: 11–13, 16).

In all our experience of church planting we have found it to be essential to make time for the core teams to do this. To meet together for worship and prayer and then to intersperse the worship and prayer with times of definite resistance towards the enemy and his dark powers. And- so what we do individually we come together to undergird and maintain corporately. In the same way, as we combine it with fasting from food or sleep on an individual basis, so we find it on the corporate basis.

Demonisation in people and how to deal with it

Mark's Gospel introduces Jesus baptised by John, anointed with the Spirit and encountering Satan. Immediately afterwards he begins to preach the gospel of the kingdom and to build the embryonic church. One of the immediate radical signs of his kingdom was that demons manifested and were cast out even inside the synagogue:

> And just then there was in their synagogue a man with an unclean spirit; and he cried out, saying, 'What do we have to do with You, Jesus of Nazareth? Have You come to destroy us? I know who You are – the Holy One of God!' And Jesus rebuked him, saying, 'Be quiet, and come out of him!' And throwing him into convulsions, the unclean spirit

cried out with a loud voice, and came out of him.
(Mk 1:23-25)

This was a first in human history. While Satan and his demons
are clearly mentioned in the Old Testament as we have seen, the
casting out of demons is hardly mentioned, if at all. Before the
coming of Jesus and his kingdom it was only just possible to
separate men and women from their sin. The sacrifice system
was only able to deal with unintentioned sin, and that only as far
as the Jews were concerned. Individual sins such as adultery and
murder were dealt with by execution. Corporate sins such as the
covetousness of Achan and his people, and the materialism,
power lust, status-seeking foulness of Egypt and the Canaanites
were dealt with by mass destruction.

Yet all along there was a glorious theme of mercy and grace
pointing forward to Christ. From Noah to Abraham, Rahab to
Nineveh; the ark, the covenant, the cord, the whale all spoke
of a way of salvation and deliverance.

It is important to realise that in the same way the Old
Testament sacrifice system was a shadow, a preparation for the
sacrifice of Christ to atone for human sin, in the same way the
executions, the battles against the Old Testament sinners and
enemies who had gone beyond the point of no return were a
shadow and a preparation for the destruction and deliverance
that Christ was to bring to and from the work of Satan. He
came to set free individuals, and to break the strongholds
which they themselves build together for the devil and his
powers (cf Heb 2:14–15).

How glad we should be that in our evangelism and church
planting today we have such a gospel and such a Jesus!
Otherwise the only remedy for inveterate sinners and
solidarities of sinners would be to protect men and women and
the future of God's kingdom by destroying such people.
Instead, by proclaiming the good name of Jesus and his
kingdom in word and action, by prayer, and by spiritual
warfare, we can see the demons uncovered and cast out!

The source and development of demonisation

It is important at this point to investigate the source and development of demonisation in individuals and solidarities of people. This will help us to discover and deal with them in our contemporary situations. In order to do so it is necessary to consider a number of very basic theological and philosophical issues.

The first cause of everything is obviously God. In that important yet rather trivial sense we can say that demonisation comes from God! This is the point the Old Testament writer makes when he refers to 'an evil spirit from the Lord' terrorising King Saul (1 Sam 16:14). But God has deliberately limited his power, what some call his sovereignty, by choosing to create human beings in his image. We are able to love him and to be his friends and colleagues although his dependent creatures. Humans are clearly not in his physical image, for God is spirit. We are therefore in his spiritual image. This deliberate decision that God has taken in creation carried the risk of the fall of the human race and of sin, sickness and death entering the world. The fall of Satan and his demons implies that they too in some way carried this image of God in spirit and were also free to turn away from him and choose darkness instead of light.

The revelation of Jesus clearly demonstrates this view of God and reality. The very concept of God becoming human, limited, a baby, in one particular time and place and family reveals this deliberate decision of his to limit himself for the sake of relationship with his people. Jesus' good news of repentance and the kingdom, his message that God is Father seeking those who will worship him in spirit and truth, and above all his unequivocal outpouring of life and love at the cross are the source for these basic theological points.

So we can say that while the first cause of demonisation is God, the immediate, the real, contemporary cause is the human sin which gives continual place to the devil. This deliberate, habitual sinning allows Satan increasing power over the life of the person and can lead ultimately to possession. This process is most vividly illustrated in the Gospel biography of Judas Iscariot, who although numbered among the apostles is first described as a practising thief (Jn 12:6), then as someone whom the devil could put things into the heart of (Jn 13:2) and eventually as someone whom Satan entered (Jn 13:27). He then, together with others who had given place to sin and Satan in the pursuit of power and status as well as money, made a stronghold for Satan and his forces in that particular time and generation as the Lord was betrayed, and Jesus and Satan met in decisive face-to-face conflict at the cross.

People can be demonised in two ways: from their own habitual sinning, like Judas, and via the destructive effects of strongholds of sin in society, such as those Judas contributed to building. These strongholds are typically encountered through the three chief social institutions: family, government and church. This is because these institutions are God-given. The family is the original context for encountering his image (Gen 1:27; 5:1-2; Mt 19:4-5); the governing authorities provide supportive and protective limits for just social interaction (Gen 11:1-9; Acts 17:26-27; Mt 22:21; Rom 13:1-7; 1 Pet 2:13-14), and church (foreshadowed in the Old Testament context by Israel) exists to provide a place where the original purpose of family and government can be salvaged and fulfilled. These are, as we have already seen, the proper spheres of angelic activity, so they are obvious contexts for satanic influence and attack.

Jesus described the Holy Spirit's activity in the age of the Kingdom as proclaiming release to captives (Lk 4:18). When the problem is a person's own habitual sinning, the answer is repentance and deliverance. Where strongholds of sin have penetrated society's defences, then healing and deliverance are mainly needed. This is not to say that there is no hurt to heal where personal sin is the chief cause, nor that there is no personal responsibility where social or structural sin has impinged. There will probably always be an element of both in each. However, we will need to prioritise either spiritual healing or moral repentance. In any case we will need to loose those involved from the domination of Satan in the name of Jesus. In both cases it is important to pinpoint the source of the problem as accurately as possible. When habitual sinning has led to demonisation, then the sin needs repenting of—as far as possible at its point of entry.

I once prayed for someone who was at what I would categorise as Judas' midway point. Not 'simply sinning' nor 'possessed', but in the situation where Satan was repeatedly able to put things into his heart. This was a sexual problem and I asked the man whether he knew when it had started. Generally, when the Holy Spirit is at work the person remembers or admits when the point was. In this case it was exposure to pornography in a particular way on a particular day years before. Repentance over that act in this person's history paved the way for deliverance from bondage.

Where a person is demonised at some level by another's damaging actions, for example in the family, the same specific disclosure is needed wherever possible. Jesus spoke clearly of the stumbling that takes place when a child or 'little one' is sinned against (Mt 18:5–7) and implied that this could lead to long-term oppression, equivalent to a millstone around the neck. He also said that the angels of such damaged people constantly behold the gaze of his Father in heaven, despite the fact that someone's sin has obscured it from them (Mt 18:10). Through uncovering the point of loss and robbery that a person has experienced, it is then possible to unloose them from the darkness and oppression that is obscuring the Father's face and to release his gaze back into their lives at the point of loss, thus ministering both healing and release.

Dealing with satanic strongholds in society

We have already seen that the process of sin and demonisation in Judas Iscariot led to the building up of satanic strongholds already existing in society. He was a thief, and this gave way to satanic oppression and possession. As a result he betrayed Jesus for money. This is precisely how demonic strongholds are formed. People who commit themselves to various forms of sin find each other and together make a place for Satan to inhabit and work from. We have also seen that the temptations of Jesus uncover and reveal the foundations of these strongholds.

The first is about the stronghold that Judas built on, the temptation to turn stones into bread: 'And the tempter came and said to Him, "If You are the Son of God, command that these stones become bread." But He answered and said, "It is written, 'Man shall not live on bread alone, but on every word that proceeds out of the mouth of God'"' (Mt 4:3–4). This temptation was simply to make getting bread more important than hearing from God; to use what power he had to feed his physical appetite instead of to hear from heaven. He was hungry, so it would not have been gluttony. Later he turns water into wine and multiplies bread and fish, so it would not have been a wrong action in principle. The wrong lay in the motive, which would have been 'my appetites and needs before God's word and God's world'. That does not even sound very bad, does it? The reason is because it is materialism, which has become one of the basic strongholds of the Western world, as it was in Israel in Jesus' day. Many of today's business enterprises, local and central government departments and other solidarities of people are merely manifestations of this stronghold.

The second and third temptations are recorded in the opposite order by Matthew and Luke – 'The devil took Him to a very high mountain, and showed Him all the kingdoms of the world, and their glory; and he said to Him, "All these things will I give You, if You fall down and worship me"' (Mt 4:8–9).

The temptation here is to desire and choose authority over other people and their families, lives and possessions for one's own glory, instead of choosing to worship God and serve his kingdom. It is important to notice here that to choose authority and glory for one's own sake is equivalent to worshipping Satan. So the choice and exercise of authority for *our* glory instead of *God's* glory is the foundation of a second satanic stronghold.

Once again, this lust for power is so normal, so much a part of the way the world functions, that it is difficult to grasp how totally wrong-footed it is. But there is no doubt about it. The disciples found difficulty in grasping this too. Even at the Last Supper they were still disputing their personal positions. In Luke 22:25–27 Jesus answered them like this:

> The kings of the Gentiles exercise lordship over them; and those in authority over them are called benefactors. But not so with you; rather let the greatest among you become as the youngest, and the leader as one who serves. For which is the greater, one who sits at table, or one who serves? Is it not the one who sits at table? But I am among you as one who serves.

This is a very basic matter, from our closest relationships with friends and family, right out through school, work, government and so on. The domination and manipulation of others for our own ends sets up a stronghold of power which is the perfect environment for demonic activity because it actually constitutes the worship of Satan. It is a complete copy of the way he operates.

In the case of the third temptation, in Luke 4:9–12, Satan took Jesus to the highest point of the temple:

> And he led Him to Jerusalem and set Him on the pinnacle of the temple, and said to Him, 'If You are the Son of God, cast Yourself down from here; for it is written, "He will give His angels charge concerning You to guard You," and, "on their hands they will bear You up, lest You strike your foot against a stone"'. And Jesus answered and said to him, 'It is said, "You shall not force a test on the Lord your God"'

This temptation was God-competition. That is to say it was the temptation to compete with God; to be the one who called the tune for God. It is really the worship of man, the attempt to submit God to man, the stronghold of jealousy and selfish ambition, the lust for status. With it Satan invited Jesus to take the highest place and to expect God to serve him in so doing. To have done so would not only have been to usurp God's place, but actually to make him the opposite kind of God to the one he is.

These anti-kingdom strongholds are fundamental to contemporary society. Money, power and status are at the centre of social and political life. In Old Testament times prophets like Amos made it clear that the point at which these anti-values held sway was the point of no return for any society. Therefore the way in which they operated had to be exposed and attacked spiritually. Amos was particularly concerned with Judah and Samaria and their six neighbours. The six neighbours formed the basis of his analysis of these strongholds in his contemporary world, which he then applied to the people of God themselves. He particularly exposed the way people were treated like things in military and economic terms; the way covenants and treaties of family and community were overturned for economic and selfish ends; the way the weak and needy were abused in terms of babies in the womb and political prisoners (Amos 1-2).

We have already seen how vital it is that the church is free from these strongholds. Jesus literally took them on in his incarnation and death, and triumphed over them in his resurrection and ascension. It is important to grasp how literally he did this. In the example of the woman at the well he put the need of the woman above his hunger. He said, 'My food is to do the will of Him who sent Me, and to accomplish His work' (Jn 4:34). Judas Iscariot, as we have already noted, betrayed him for money. On the cross he refused the drug which would have spared him the reality of the battle. Jesus overcame the stronghold of materialism there. In the example of the feeding of the five thousand Jesus put prayer above the offer of people power: 'Jesus therefore perceiving that they were intending to come and take Him by force, to make Him king, withdrew again to the mountain by Himself alone'. (Jn 6:15).

At the cross he declined to call on angelic help to defeat his enemies by means of military power: 'Do you think that I cannot appeal to My Father, and He will at once put at My disposal more than twelve legions of angels?' (Mt 26:53). Jesus overcame the stronghold of human power there. Finally, in the example of his relatives urging him to show off his divinity in Jerusalem, he refused, and put his humble dependence on God's timing before public status and position. At the cross he refused to rise to the taunts that he should come down off the cross and save himself if he were the Son of God. Jesus overcame the stronghold of status and position there. In the words of Paul, at the cross Jesus 'disarmed the rulers and authorities' (Col 2:15). As the Holy Spirit guides us, we too must take on these strongholds and win in the same divine power.

In the early 1980s God showed us that the same analysis made by Amos applied to our contemporary society. The readiness to kill the innocent with the guilty for political and economic purposes by the use of nuclear armaments; the easy breaking of political treaties and marriage covenants for economic and selfish expediency; the proliferation of abortion and the failure to act on behalf of the oppressed—all this brought Western society under the judgement of God. These things were strongholds that we needed to expose and attack spiritually.

We set about a campaign at local and national levels to deal with these issues as the Holy Spirit led us, and this still continues. These anti-kingdom strongholds are the real powers, the real depths of Satan, which, if left unchecked, give free rein to the kinds of immorality and occultism that ultimately overtook Sodom and Gomorrah, ancient Egypt and Babylon, and will be the ultimate doom of the contemporary 'Babylon' now emerging in Europe and the USA.

In 1987 we encountered the blatant approval and promotion of homosexual practice increasingly rife in our society. We knew we had to face it and deal with it spiritually. Let me state unequivocally that homosexual orientation is an expected and growing result of a society lost in the terms that Paul describes in the second half of Romans 1. Such folk need love, compassion, repentance and healing, not condemnation, marginalisation and fear. But the setting up of strongholds of homosexual practice and promotion under the guise of civil rights has to be exposed and opposed in spiritual warfare and prophetic action as the Holy Spirit leads.

We were led to gather together the support of more than thirty local evangelical churches in the Lewisham Borough (we had not realised there were so many!) and make representations to the local borough council. When these were ignored we leafleted 89,000 households with the council's proposals for allowing practising homosexuals to form an increasing stronghold in the borough. There is still a spiritual battle to fight. But we thank God that he has helped us to shift something real and provide a base for greater victory in the UK on this front.

The big problem of the Western church is that it is often subverted by the political right or left. But we need to be the servants of justice as well as personal morality. As we faced the morality issue of homosexual practice, the Lord showed us that we needed many more social justice projects in the London boroughs in which we were working. As a result we established and are multiplying many such projects; among the homeless, the elderly, the unemployed and so on. We have seen the need to encourage the formation of united fraternals of living Christians across the churches to provide a spiritual frontline of positive relationships with local authorities, as well as a vehicle for social and political action. These projects and fraternals are prophetic acts of spiritual warfare against the strongholds of money, power and status. Our 'small' local actions and attempts to take on national and international Goliaths are all part of the unseen warfare which God is increasingly using to dethrone Satan in our generation.

As it was with Jesus, so it will be with us, as we trust him and follow his way in evangelism and church planting. He dealt with the principalities and powers. So must we. As he reached out together with others to plant his church, the demons manifested and he cast them out. So must we. As he dealt with the demonised individuals, Jesus increasingly encountered the satanic strongholds, and on the cross He broke their power. Consequently the church was planted and grew. So it will be with us.

PART 2

MODELS AND STRUCTURE

CHAPTER 5

MODELS OF CHURCH PLANTING

by Roger Forster

> All authority in heaven and on earth has been given to me. Therefore go and make disciples of all nations, baptising them in the name of the Father and of the Son and of the Holy Spirit, and teaching them to obey everything I have commanded you. And surely I will be with you always, to the very end of the age (Mt. 28:18–20).

Jesus gave his followers the commission to go and make disciples of all nations. He instructed them to teach these new disciples everything that they themselves had been taught, and his emphasis is important: it is not *some* things, not, 'All things, but some are in brackets because they don't apply any more', but, 'Everything I have commanded you.' This would, of course, include the commission that had already been given to them, namely to go and heal the sick, cast out demons and preach the good news to the poor – the rich had better come and get it themselves! However, the discipleship training for the future church was not to stop there at Matthew 10: it was to cover every aspect of Jesus' teaching.

The fundamental implication of this comprehensive commission is that whatever we need to know about church-planting must somewhere or other be embryonic in Jesus' own teaching. Jesus would not have given his disciples the task of world evangelism, of world discipling, without providing them with the necessary know-how to get the job done. It becomes manifestly clear that the first disciples used the strategy of church planting to set about the job Jesus had given them. The job was to produce total, radical disciples – such were the only sort of disciples Jesus talked about making. These disciples were to be in all nations throughout the world.

In certain circles it is hardly worth making the assertion that the way to world evangelism is church planting because it is so generally accepted. However, there are still certain pockets of resistance, of conservatism and traditionalism, which do not go back far enough to the radicalism of the New Testament. Believers from these pockets still seem to find it rather hard to believe that world evangelism is going to be accomplished by planting churches. The strategy of planting churches, however, must have been implicit in Jesus' teaching, and it was certainly explicit in the Acts of the Apostles as the first disciples proceeded to obey the Lord, otherwise they would not have immediately planted churches in order to fulfil the Great Commission.

Some Statistics

In the USA the fastest growing denomination is a conservative but very missionary orientated denomination with top priority on world evangelisation. Some might attribute the exciting growth of this church to its conservative, historic, orthodox, fundamentalist, Bible-believing tradition, but the facts speak to the contrary. Those churches of the denomination which have not produced new churches, or are not themselves new churches, are declining at exactly the same rate as the fastest declining American denomination. The only reason why the first denomination is the fastest growing is because it has churches which are producing churches, producing churches, producing churches, etc. That is where the fantastic, numerical increase is taking place. Where a denomination has stopped planting churches it will decline, and it will decline at almost a common, regular rate. Where churches are structured to reproduce themselves, then that particular movement, or flow, or group of churches will continue to grow.

In October 1989 a census, known as the English Church Census, was taken in England in an attempt to measure as precisely as possible the number of people attending church on one particular Sunday. It was probably the most in-depth church survey that has ever been held, and encompassed all the different churchmanships – evangelical, liberal, catholic, etc. It has provided some very concrete statistics to start to analyse where the church in England is at today.

The survey showed that in England 10% of the population are regular church-goers. For the purposes of the census the churches they attended were categorised into three main streams: the Roman Catholic Church was the best attended of the three streams, but attendance had declined at a rate of 14% over five years. The Free Churches constituted the second largest of the streams, and they were shown to be increasing at a very modest rate of 2 – 3% over five years. The Anglican Church was shown to be declining by 8% over five years. The survey demonstrated, however, that one branch of the church was sustaining dramatic growth right across Britain: the new and independent churches, which belong to a simpler, biblical commitment and are largely charismatic churches, had grown in size by 144%.

The first conclusion we can draw is that it is churches which reproduce churches that are growing in committed membership. In a continent where the church is not growing, there is evidence that a certain type of church is on a growth curve of around 144%, and these are churches with structures that facilitate change. In another five years the attendance of the new churches will probably more than double. We may not like this trend; we may have ecumenical aspirations that want to disregard it; we may have theological objections based, for example, upon Jesus' words, "I pray that they may be one;" but we cannot deny the simple facts.

I believe that in Europe we have to be prepared to be radical enough to ask the question, 'Why is it that after two thousand years we have not yet fulfilled that obvious, straightforward Great Commission of Jesus?' Jesus said, "My yoke is easy", and we should have been able to fulfil the task he set us, but two thousand years later something has obviously gone wrong. I want to suggest that what has gone wrong is that we have stopped planting. The church is growing in every other continent of the world, but in these places they plant churches and are not hindered by an archaic parish system.

Informality – a key

Looking at church planting from a slightly different perspective, we see that there are some theologians who say that Jesus didn't set up a church at all. Of course, these liberals dismiss the fact that he did say, "I will build my church," and that there is one other passage, in Matthew 18, where he used the word 'church'. They would probably say that these words were put into the mouth of Jesus later, and they would thus excise these verses in favour of their blanket statement. These theologians hold the view that Jesus did not intend to set up a great institution called the church: he came to teach us how to love one another; how to have peace in our hearts and be peacemakers, sons of God; how to know what it is to be poor in spirit and, therefore, filled with God's presence. Jesus wasn't into 'churchianity', they say; rather it was the Apostle Paul who introduced churchianity. Although we know that liberalism is too destructive, many of us find our hearts rising up and saying, "Yes, that God, at last!" Of course Jesus walked under the trees of Galilee, he got fishermen out of their boats, he never owned a building, or put a spire on a church; he just lived. That is the kind of Christianity we want to get into. That very overstatement of the liberals has enough truth to it for us to begin to say to ourselves that maybe the critics are putting their finger on something important for church life and church growth.

Perhaps the hub of the matter is not that Jesus did not set up a church, but that the kind of church he instituted was nothing like the sort of churches that are all over the world today. His was a church that could actually do the job that he had commanded it to do – to make disciples of all the nations. Clearly the churches we have today are not those sorts of churches, because they have not done the job. No church today has the answer, otherwise our mission would by now have been fulfilled. When we do find the answer, the task will get done.

So, the Lord came and taught us by his own example, and a keynote of his church was informality. It was a church in which there was room for the wind of God, a church where things could keep changing to meet changing situations. Informality is the first emphasis that seems to flow out of the kind of church that Jesus was bringing into being under the trees of Galilee, by the lakeside and in the mountains of Judea. It is this sort of church, then, that Jesus expected would evangelise the world: the sort that he founded and provided for his disciples and expected them to reproduce in obedience to him.

The hierarchies of authoritarian structures that exist in many churches are the greatest hindrance, practically and theologically speaking, to the release of the colossal energy and power that God wants to put into old men who dream, young men who have visions, and sons and daughters who prophesy. The essential feature of this new people that was coming into being, called the church of Jesus Christ, was that it was a people's movement. It was not just made up of the elite Gideons, or Samsons, or Davids, who were blessed with the Spirit of God, but of the whole people being saturated and blessed with the outpoured Spirit. The impact of God's presence within this kind of church would be so powerful that it would break out through every single corpuscle and cell into fulfilling the task of world evangelism. The instrument that Jesus ordains for world evangelisation is informal and free, and must be able to throw off the heavy, structural hierarchical systems which prevent it doing what Jesus taught it to do. Sentimental traditionalism and false views of unity must not be allowed to lull us into paying lip service to an invention that has nothing whatsoever to do with Jesus' mind, just because it happens to call itself a church. The Lord is not going to ask us at the end of the days, "Were you true to something that I never invented?" He is going to ask, "Were you true to what I was setting up, what I was doing, and were you willing to get into a position where you could get my commandment done?" A false sense of loyalty to something which is other than Jesus is preventing the church, again and again, from getting on with the task of obeying him in taking the good news to all the world.

Based on relationships

Secondly, at the heart of this aspect of informality is relationships. The bottom line of what church is all about is relationships between people in the Holy Spirit. When Jesus began to set up the church, he gathered twelve men around himself, and they entered into relationship with him and each other. As they travelled together as a kind of mobile body, a mobile church, they were building deeper and deeper not only their relationships into him, but their relationships into each other, because he was in them as well.

Compare Jesus' approach with some of our own strategies for church planting. Jesus did not set about raising enough money out of his disciples in Galilee to buy the temple building from Caiaphas, so that they could then all move in and start the new church. Nor did he set out to discredit Caiaphas as a false high priest, to have him put out of office, in order to be able to take over and declare himself the real high priest. He might have argued that, having done away with the established ecclesiastical structures, he and his disciples could then become the best vehicle for the business of winning people. Nor did Jesus seek to take on himself the God-given traditions of Israel and attempt to demonstrate that he was the fulfilment of it all, in such a way that the whole of the history of Israel could now flow into his hand and he would use it powerfully to reach the people. Rather, Jesus gathered a bunch of apostles around him, and commanded them to go out and do the same.

And that was exactly what they did:" they gathered a bunch of 3,000 at Pentecost, then 5,000 and so it went on. The Apostle Paul worked in the same way, and everywhere he went, he didn't say, "Get a building, get a doctrinal statement, get ...". He said, "Get together," and that was the church. In the letter to the Ephesians, the great church epistle, the Greek prefix *sun* meaning 'together' occurs twelve times: together-body, together-seated, together-raise ... It is the togetherness of those who love Jesus and want to get near him that constitutes the church. That is why the informality that Jesus is accused of is fundamental to church life because its life is based upon relationships. That is the kind of church that is going to accomplish world evangelisation. We will evangelise the world by doing it Jesus' way, with bunches of people all over the earth living out the incarnated life of Jesus Christ so that people can see the good news. We need to plant out more and more churches, so that everywhere we go we trip over them. Not just one in a town, but dozens of them all over the place, different shapes, different sizes, but so that wherever people go they find church, Jesus' body, and see Jesus.

If every church in the world today – and by that I mean a local congregation – reproduced itself three times by the year 2000 we would have a church, a body of people, in every thousand people in the world. I would envisage the church being about 130 people in size. Instead of being satisfied because there is a good church seven miles down the road, we can think in terms of planting at least fourteen churches before we get to it!

Culturally relevant

A vital possibility within the context of every new body of people that keeps springing into being every couple of years or even every half a year, is the potential within that informal group of relationships to express Jesus in the cultural norms out of which those people have been converted. We no longer leave our gift at the altar and go and get right with our brother, because the altar was an object taken from the culture of Jesus' day and so he is teaching from the first-century Jewish situation. The valley of Gehinom means nothing to us. Gehenna is a culturally clothed expression which has to be explained as the local council rubbish tip before it begins to make sense. We would use a totally different expression today. So in current terminology we might say, "If you are angry in your heart you will be in danger of ending up at the tip." It is not incumbent upon the church of today to adopt the cultural connotations of two thousand years ago. The church today needs to be as culturally relevant as Jesus was to his own culture. We need churches that have been stripped of their non-cultural relevance, and I am not just referring to buildings. A single-parent mum pushes her pram past the great closed oak doors of a church and wonders what goes on in there, but she would never dare to find out. We must stop playing at religion and start getting Jesus expressed in the earth. We have to be radical and plant culturally relevant churches all over the place, just as Jesus himself was culturally relevant in his own day.

God in a hurry

Many Christians seem to believe that God is not in a hurry to get his purposes accomplished on the earth, but if God is long-suffering it is for one reason only: he has committed himself to his wayward bride. Instead of letting her go, he has stuck by her as she has taken wrong paths, wrong locations and spoken wrong expressions for two thousand years, while all the time he has been trying to woo and draw her back into his ways. The Bible actually teaches that God is not slow (2 Pet 3:9), and "the King's business requires haste" (1 Sam 21:8). In the New Testament we are taught, "God is not slow concerning his promises." Yet God wants all to come to repentance, and is waiting for the good news to be preached in all the world. His slowness is due to our slowness: his hurrying is that he wants his promises to be fulfilled. His hurry should become ours (2 Pet 3:12). God is committed 100% to getting glory to his Son until the earth resounds and redounds to the glory of God, responding to his presence (Phil 2:5–11).

A reproducing church

All species, as they mature, have the ability for reproduction. Within the structures of the sort of church I have been describing there is inherent the ability for reproduction. There is a womb structured within it. So, if a church exists which never thinks about reproducing itself, never talks about, never plans, prepares, trains for it, never exhorts its people to it, never expects or anticipates that this is the natural business of growing up, then it is actually sterile.

God delights in the great variety of peoples that exist in the world: male, female, black, white, brown, yellow, red .... He must do because he created us all. No one type of human being is the *pièce de résistance*, and the same is also true of the church. The different streams of churches will have different characteristics; individual churches will emphasise and express things in different ways. There is plenty of evidence in the New Testament to suggest that there are different structures and patterns of church life. Jerusalem was not at all like Corinth. In Jerusalem they broke bread from house to house; in Corinth they all had to wait until they came together: a clear difference in structure. In Thessalonica they despised prophesying, in Corinth they never stopped. We too should expect different expressions of church life: variety within the species. That is why we don't want to squeeze everybody into our particular mould. We want the Spirit of God to be doing lots of new and reproductive things in our churches.

Eight New Testament models of church planting

In the New Testament eight different models for church planting can be seen from what was happening in the Acts of the Apostles. It does not mean that if you believe God is leading you into one model, you cannot use the others, because often they interact with each other. Each of these models is hinted at and seen embryonically in the life and teaching of Jesus. As we look at each in turn, we will consider both the relevant Acts passage and the embryonic seed in Jesus and his teaching and example.

1. Mass evangelism church plant

The first model is the mass evangelism church plant. Some would think it totally incongruous that mass evangelism could be used for planting a church, but I believe it could be harnessed for this purpose if the organisations sought to incorporate within their working framework structures which would facilitate church planting. This is what Peter did in Acts 2, when his three thousand converts were first baptised, and then "they broke bread from house to house, remaining in the apostolic doctrine, eating their meat with gladness and singleness of heart" (Acts 2:42); and so the church began to grow in its house units as well as in its mass rallies in Solomon's porch.

I believe the effectiveness of mass evangelism would change overnight if evangelists built into their follow-up systems at least the possibility of planting a church out of their converts. Following the last Billy Graham mission in London, we found a much better success rate than usual of assimilating converts into our own particular church – 38%. However, in another campaign, we encountered problems in this area. A statement by the organisers indicated that the equivalent of eighty-seven new churches of average size had come out of the campaign, but sadly it was attempted to integrate converts into existing structures and many of them were killed and lost there. It should come as no surprise to find that new Christians have difficulty growing in a mortuary! Eighty-seven new churches in London would have provoked enquiry; converts assimilated or lost do not.

In Mark 6, Jesus was undertaking some 'mass evangelism' when he taught the crowd of five thousand men plus women and children. In verse 39 Jesus "commanded them to make all sit down by companies on the green grass". Jesus very thoughtfully wanted them to sit and recline where it was comfortable, on the green grass – not on the dry dust – and he sat them down in 'ranks' or 'flower beds', or so it could be translated, by one hundreds and by fifties. The word used for 'companies' is 'symposium', *sym* together, *posium* to drink. They were drinking parties looking like bunches of flowers, in hundreds and fifties.

So, right from the beginning, the Lord's mass evangelism had a structure in it to plant groups, companies, bodies of people. And I still believe that that kind of mass evangelism has a Christ-rooted basis, and an Acts of the Apostles' precedent which we can still use today.

Two of the most outstanding evangelists of the inter-war period were the Jeffreys brothers; they were the products of the Welsh revival, full of Welsh fervour and the Holy Spirit's power. They moved from town to town, and after being thrown out of most of the denominational churches, they set up their tent, carried their baptistry with them, and then masses of people came to them because they were praying for the sick and seeing them healed. They baptised them on the spot when they professed conversion. They then set up groups and that is how they planted the Elim denomination, which grew at great speed between the wars. That is mass evangelism being used for church planting.

For mass evangelism to be fully effective, the desire for church planting must be incorporated into the heart and structure of the work.

2. The mega-church plant

Now the mega-church is what happened in Jerusalem. In chapter 6 of Acts we see the church in Jerusalem getting bigger and bigger. All the original Galilean believers had moved down to Jerusalem (John was the only one who due to his well-to-do background, was more likely to have a house there already from which his fish could be sold). The church was big enough to support the twelve apostles who were giving the best possible teaching, and there were enough resources to initiate a social action programme (Acts 6:1–6) looking after the widows. The church in Jerusalem may have grown to 40,000 before the persecution came, and that is the next stage of development in the mega-church pattern.

So the mega–church in Jerusalem was a place where its members had received the best possible teaching; where the twelve were training up people to take their place – mini apostles like Stephen and Phillip; where wonderful healings were taking place and people were being saved. This potential for teaching, training, social action and exposure to the power of the Holy Spirit could never be available in a small, backwater fellowship. But then the persecution comes, and suddenly the whole of Judea is evangelised, as the church is scattered and congregations come into being all over the country.

This is an effective model for the evangelisation of a small country or a given region with a good control city or town. Move all the Christians into the centre, give them the best possible teaching, and then tell them to go back home and put it into practice there. Persecution as an added incentive to dispersion might be a little more difficult to arrange!

I believe this model has its roots in Jesus' own teaching. As he went up towards Jerusalem, the Lord was gathering around him an ever-bigger and bigger crowd. For the eight months before his entry into Jerusalem, he travelled from Caesarea Philippi, right through Galilee, around Samaria into Perea, over to the other side of the Jordan, then across the river at Jericho and up towards Jerusalem. He was attracting a great crowd of those who had come to love and trust him, and those who wanted to know more about him. This culminated in his triumphal entry into Jerusalem, where masses of people came out to greet him and crowds of others followed him in, with the result that he had drawn into Jerusalem a large crowd of his adherents.

At the Last Supper, Jesus said: "They will smite the shepherd and the sheep will be scattered, but ..." (Mk 14:27). Now, when they were scattered, they would go back to where they had come from, mainly Galilee. But Jesus had also said, "I will go before you into Galilee" (14:28), and the word for 'go' is the same as is used for 'the shepherd going before the sheep'. So, he would go and collect them from Galilee, but what would happen next? He would bring them back to Jerusalem. It was Jesus' instigation (cf, Lk 24; Mt 28; Jn21; Mk 16; Acts 1) that brought them out of Galilee back to Jerusalem to wait for the Holy Spirit and for the first great mega-church to come into being. The building of the mega-Jerusalem church was implicit in Jesus' own prophetic words in Mark 14:28: "I will go before you to Galilee" in order that he would lead them back having been scattered, to Jerusalem.

Of course, Yonggi Cho's church in Korea is, perhaps the foremost example of the mega-church. Korea, where just over 100 years ago there were no churches at all, now has the three largest churches in the world. Big churches can do big things, like buying a mountain to establish a prayer mountain with its tremendous impact on Korea and the whole world, but don't be suprised if the big church suddenly gets broken up and scattered throughout the earth to get the job of planting churches done.

3. The maybe church plant

The third model of church plant has the unusual name of the maybe church. This describes a group of people already assembling for some religious/spiritual purpose and who are already relating to each other to some degree. For instance, in Acts 10 Peter encounters Cornelius Christians, but realises, "I see that God has no respect for persons, but accepts those in every nation who fear him and do justly." They are soon converted, baptised and filled with the Spirit, and the first maybe church becomes a church plant.

A similar process occurs when Paul meets Lydia and her prayer group in Acts 16, and again when he comes across a group of John the Baptist's followers in Acts 19. The foundations for conversion had already been laid in the lives of John's disciples, and Paul asks them, "Did you receive the Holy

Spirit when you believed?" and then in the power of the Holy Spirit brought them right through to a total experience of life in Jesus Christ.

This truth is illustrated in the life of Jesus as the disciples of John leave him to follow Jesus (Jn 1). John the Baptist himself acknowledges: "I must decrease; he must increase" (Jn 3:30).

In Richardson's book *Eternity in Their Hearts* there are stories of various tribal situations which had long-held traditions that one day someone would come who would bring them the truth. Eventually, a missionary or other Christian did indeed arrive and with them the fulfilment of their centuries-old legend.

Today, in England, there has been a most unusual movement of the Holy Spirit among Christadelphians over the last six or seven years. Christadelphians do not believe in the deity of Jesus Christ, but the Holy Spirit has touched many of their groups, with the result that whole companies, or sections, have become Christians. Something similar has happened among Jehovah's Witnesses, and converts are going back into the system to bring their good news to others.

It may be that God will want to call some Christians to be on the lookout for groups of this kind, where there is a sincere and open searching. Their meeting-place might even be a mosque, as we know of some such groups, but in reality they are seeking to woship Jesus. Others could be seekers from New Age societies who have never really been confronted with the real Jesus We have heard of a huge movement of deficient Christianity in China where hundreds have now come to Christ by their leader meeting a vital evangelist while both were in prison. God may want to lead Christians to dedicate themselves to situations like these, to pray and seek to bring them through into true faith and experience so that the maybe church may become a church plant.

4. The mushroom church plant

In Acts 11 the Antioch church came into being, not because the apostles or the great leaders of the church decided to have a church there, but because the ordinary everyday Christians chatted about Jesus, and Gentiles got converted. The apostles put them together in church life because they didn't know what else to do with them. So it was that ordinary Christians were planting these mushroom churches.

Why call them mushroom churches? "Because the wind blows where it wills and you hear the sound thereof" (Jn 3:9), but you cannot control it, and so it is with the Holy Spirit. The Holy Spirit blows the spores and that is how mushrooms spread. The Spirit of God will not be controlled by ecclesiastical hierarchies, and mushroom churches will come into being and, dare I suggest, even the apostles could not control it.

> Jesus and his disciples had had a hard week or so of missioning, and the Master suggested: "Come yourselves apart and rest awhile in a desert place and there were many coming and going, and they had no leisure so much as to eat and they departed into a desert place by ship, and the people saw them departing and many knew them and ran afoot together thither, out of the cities, and got there ahead of him. When Jesus landed and saw a large crowd he had compassion on them, because they were like sheep without a shepherd. So he began teaching them many things" (Mk: 32–34.)

Even Jesus did not control the movement of the people. His intention was rest, but much to his disciples' chagrin, he saw the need of the people and went on working. Later, in Acts, it was the Spirit of God who was again in control and was well able to spawn off Antioch when even the hierarchy in Jerusalem were not aware of what was going on. Of course they did have a part to play in blessing them and giving them leadership in the shape of Barnabas and later Saul. So Antioch was a mushrooming influence.

It is important to notice the incident when John, after stopping a man casting out demons in the name of Jesus, came to Jesus and with a touch of pride explained what he had done. Jesus replied, "No one who does a miracle in my name can in the next moment say anything bad about me, for whoever is not against us is with us" (Mk 9:39–40). So often we want to control the person who is not one of us, but has none the less been blessed and is using Jesus' name in power. We should instead be saying, "You go for it because you are with us." It is true that Jesus also said, "He that is not with me is against me" (Mt 12:30), but there he is putting the emphasis on himself personally, whereas in our verse above it is the relationship of the preacher to the church which is in view.

There is a lovely story of the Welshman, Reverend Thomas, who, about a hundred years ago, tried to take Bibles into Korea. When his boat arrived, he was not allowed to get off but, as he watched, two Jesuit priests disembarked and were immediately put to death. The boat sailed on a bit further, and got stuck on a sandbank with Thomas aboard. The Koreans set fire to a junk and pushed it into the current. Thomas' boat was hit, went up in flames and everybody had to abandon ship. As they reached shore, the shipwrecked people were murdered by the Koreans. In a last ditch attempt Thomas offered his Bibles to his assassinator who tore them to shreds and threw the paper into the air. The papers scattered everywhere, the locals picked them up and used them to build a house. People who came along were able to read on the walls of the house things such as, "For God so loved the world that he gave his only Son ...", and so when missionaries got to Korea a few years later there was a church already waiting. That is a mushroom church.

5. A mobile church plant

Acts 13 is a mobile team church plant. Paul gathers together a small group of people, including Mark and Barnabas, moves into an area and sets about the work of planting a church. When the church is established, they move on. The number of people in the mobile team varies in size, but in Acts 20 there are perhaps as many as fifteen people travelling with him. The length of time Paul stayed in various localities is worth noting:

he stayed three years in Ephesus, eighteen months in Corinth, and two years in Rome.

A variation of this method of planting churches would be actually to set up teams that are specifically trained in the work of church planting, so that they would move from town to town leaving a church behind at each place. The famous Celtic missionary movement was an example of this strategy. Working in teams of twelve, based on the Lord's model – with some, but by no means all, celibate team members – a team would move into an area, live and share together for two to three years and by the time they moved on they had established a church in that locality.

Perhaps it is time for our denominations to set aside groups of people to go and attempt the task of planting churches. With a minibus, rucksacks, a supply of food and, perhaps, a tent, a project could soon be on the road. A team could set up in an area, work there for an allotted period of time and then move on, once a church was sufficiently independent.

This was, of course, the way in which Jesus himself worked, gathering a team about him and together forming a mobile church, living, sharing, loving and caring for one another. Those who observed them would want to participate in their way of life and would be drawn into the family. It can be the same today too so that when people see the mini-church, the mini-body in action in the team life of a mobile body of people, they want to get in on the act, and then they get converted.

6. The mini-mission church plant

When Paul arrives in Corinth in Acts 18, he comes across Aquila and Priscilla, a couple who had been pushed out of Rome by Claudius because they were Jews (and probably Jewish Christian already), because of the "instigation of Chrestus", almost certainly a misunderstanding by the Roman authorities of the cause of disturbances in the Jewish quarter. The preaching of Jesus as Christ disturbed the status quo, not a Greek slave called Chrestus. Aquila and Priscilla open their home to their fellow tent-maker Paul and get involved in the work of church planting. They are absolutely 100% essential for the planting of the Corinthian church. Later, this same couple are to be found in Ephesus, and then in Rome, and in each situation the church is based in their house.

The Watchman Nee movement in China saw some 700 churches come into being within ten years! Their most usual method of church planting was to pick out a couple from the church who were committed, taught and ready to move with their family, preferably together with one or two other couples, and send them to the next town. They would settle in, try to get a job – doing whatever they could because they were not in life for a career, but for seeing the church expand – and within a few months they would have collected around them a few interested people. Then Watchman Nee and his fellow apostles would come in, teach the people and establish a church. That was one of the fastest ways of church growth before the revolution in China.

I believe Jesus had this kind of pattern in mind when he made Capernaum his headquarters and did a great deal of his work in that area before he began his missions. Jesus sent the disciples out in pairs and they stayed in homes in the different villages that he himself was going to come to at a later date. This was a way of establishing units and groups in each of the societal units/communities that existed. And surely the home of Martha, Mary and Lazarus in Bethany must have been a hot-bed for church planting with people coming into the home, seeing Jesus when he was there and getting blessed, and that incidentally is probably where the disciples fled at the time of the crucifixion.

7. The mother church plant

A very important church-plant method is the mother church and her daughters. It is perhaps best illustrated by Ephesus. During the period of three years when Paul stayed in Ephesus not only was a strong central church built up, but we know that certainly Colosse, Hierapolis and Laodicea also came into being. Although Paul had never visited Colosse, he was able to write to the Christians there as if they were his own church, and this is because it was spawned by the mother church at Ephesus as, in all probability, were all the churches of the Book of Revelation: Smyrna, Pergamum, Thyatira, etc. They circle around Ephesus and they probably all came into being because of the strong Ephesian church: a mother church planting bits of church back into the outlying towns and villages.

This method is one we have used in Ichthus in London to great effect. We began as one congregation in the south-east corner of London, and remained like that for eight years, but now, after a further nine years, there are forty congregations. This is the concept of the mother church spawning her daughters, but the process has not occurred once only, because now some of those daughters have become mother churches in their own right. At first the 'baby' church remains a part of the mother's body, but then the baby becomes a separate unity, dependent on the mother to some degree, until eventually it gains total independence. This is perhaps the fastest way to plant congregations and that is what we would love to see happening right across England, not just with Ichthus churches – but if nobody else will do it, some of us will have to!

The four places where the lists of apostles whom Jesus chose occur set out the names in three groups of four. The groups themselves are always in the same sequence, but within the groups the order is always different, although the group leader is always the same one. If the lists of apostles in the Gospels and in the Acts are placed alongside each other, it becomes clear that numbers one, five and nine are always the same person, and numbers two/three/four, six/seven/eight, ten/eleven/twelve are always grouped together but these are in a different order, so that there are the same three groups of four. Within the twelve apostles there is already structure growing up in readiness for spreading out and forming new bodies. They are already naturally building their relationships so that when the time comes to plant out, they will be ready. I believe this was part of the plan Jesus had in mind. So a church based on house groups already has relationships structured ready for the next plant. It is as though each church body should have a womb in it, ready for reproduction.

8. The multi-cell church plant

In Acts 28 we see the Apostle Paul in his own hired house, using a home-base to teach the Jews who come to him about Jesus and the kingdom of God. This is a more private approach to church planting. Even before Paul arrived there were already at least five households of believers established in Rome. In Romans 16 there are five groups mentioned, which some people identify as one church, others as five churches and others as still more churches, but I don't think it really matters: church is church is church. Structures can be organised in various ways, with, for example, either a number of congregations each having their own leaders or a large congregation having a group of leaders. The important thing is that the body life is functioning effectively. Suffice it to say that in Romans 16 there are various identifiable groups: in verses 3 and 5 Priscilla and Aquila, and the church in their home; in verse 10 Aristobulus' household; in verse 11, the household of Narcissus, and in verse 14 the brothers and verse 15 the saints with them.

It is possible to plant churches simply by having house groups. This is a particularly effective method in countries where the regime is very anti-Christian. It has become known that before the war in the Middle East there was a very large number of cell groups coming into being, with many of them not even knowing of each other's existence. This provides an element of safety. It illustrates a cellular-style church life. In the situation in Rome although the groups knew of each other, they were not highly organised. Ralph Neighbour has written a whole book on this particular style, *Where Do We Go From Here?* Something of this method is displayed in Jesus' ministry when in Mark's Gospel he is found ten times in homes, conducting a meeting of some kind. This is a cellular church.

These eight styles of church planting, each practised at various times in the Acts of Apostles and each with its roots in Jesus' teaching, provide the church with the procedures it needs to get on with the task of fulfilling the Great Commission. We can choose to use just one of the methods, or however many help us to engage in the task. We need, however, to grasp hold of the truth that Jesus, the best teacher the world has ever known, has given us all we need to know, and now the church must get on with the job as quickly as possible so that the task might be fulfilled in our generation!

Happy church planting!

CHAPTER 6

A SLICE OF DYNAMIC CHURCH LIFE

The scene was set. An interdenominational grouping of evangelists working from a para-church base. It was a consultation and brain-storming session intended to grapple with some of the difficult issues related to the ongoing discipleship and integration of new converts, particularly young people, into church.

Disappointments were expressed with regard to the follow-up rates and lack of ongoing fruit after big crusades. Complaints were aired with regard to the reluctance of many established churches to be flexible enough to integrate new people. More depressing, all kinds of mutant discipleship models were being suggested. One evangelist even proposed the setting up of 'halfway house' churches which would slowly domesticate converts into the ways of the established churches after which they could be integrated. What use they would be after 'domestication' no one was prepared to estimate. It was at this stage that I suggested what appeared to be a novel idea. Perhaps church and church planting were the natural and biblical context and model for discipleship and evangelism. Perhaps the only way to break into new areas and strata of our society is seriously to consider the planting of new Great Commission communities whose focus will be on those outside the church rather than maintaining the status quo. Maybe new wineskins were needed for new wine. Hardly a new nor radical suggestion from my perspective!

However, many will be unable to cope with this premise because the mention of church planting in some circles immediately seems to be a threat to existing churches, sometimes because of denominational policy (eg the parish system) or the feeling of competition.

By contrast, others, regardless of persuasion have already seized this vision with enthusiasm.

My own perspective is that in a nation where more than 85% of people are unchurched, and less than 10% of people are in church, we could do with as many new churches as possible. It is not an issue of competition, but rather of partnership in order to get the job done. In fact church growth experts estimate that to network the gospel effectively we need an active, proclaiming church for every 1,000 of the community. By this reckoning we have a long way to go worldwide: about seven million churches according to DAWN 2000!

Something strange has happened in past generations. It seems that the work of evangelism and mission has had to be done outside of the church context. No doubt the inflexibility of many churches has pushed pioneers in this direction. However, in our church planting we need to ensure that we are building the foundations of a different 'animal': a church that will see itself as an agent of God's cosmic purpose, whose vision is outward and which is preoccupied with its calling and destiny

In this chapter I want to do a cross-section of the life of the growing church. There is no space for a thorough doctrinal analysis of church, but I want to outline some key biblical perspectives which show us that the church is not outmoded, outdated or irrelevant. In its New Testament form it is the heaven sent, designed and built vehicle for God's purposes. The biblical records of the early church are both a challenge to the contemporary church and also a comfort. It appears that even they had their problems. These records show us that under God's mighty hand the early Christian communities grew rapidly in both size and influence. They flourished in the apostolic teaching, the outpouring of the Holy Spirit and a rich community experience.

> They devoted themselves to the apostles' teaching and to the fellowship, to the breaking of bread and to prayer. Everyone was filled with awe, and many wonders and miraculous signs were done by the apostles. All the believers were together and had everything in common. Selling their possessions and goods, they gave to anyone as he had need. Every day they continued to meet together in the temple courts. They broke bread in their homes and ate together with glad and sincere hearts, praising God and enjoying the favour of all the people. And the Lord added to their number daily those who were being saved (Acts 2:42–47).

There appeared to be no normative pattern or structure to the church's life. Different models emerged both within Jewish and Gentile communities. These reflected the same leadership principles and character (1 Tim 3; Tit 1:5) which were expressed somewhat differently in the varied cultural contexts (Acts 15:1-35). The development of these communities was strategic, as can be seen from their early focus on key cities like Jerusalem, Antioch, Corinth and Ephesus. Yet it was dynamic and Spirit-led (Acts 16:6–10), and it reveals a fluid structure which developed continually as growth demanded rapid change (Acts 6:1–7).

Fully proclaiming the gospel

Roger Forster often refers to the characteristics of the Pauline church foundations. One of those he highlights is drawn from Romans 15:17-20:

> Therefore I glory in Christ Jesus in my service to God. I will not venture to speak of anything except what Christ has accomplished through me in leading the Gentiles to obey God by what I have said and done – by the power of signs and miracles, through the power of the Spirit. So from Jerusalem all the way around to Illyricum, I have fully proclaimed the gospel of Christ. It has always been my ambition to preach the gospel where Christ was not known, so that I would not be building on someone else's foundation.

Revealed here is not just a glimpse of the type of gospel Paul, and by inference his churches, was proclaiming, but also an important characteristic of this proclamation: that is, fully proclaiming. Paul considers his work in these regions completed, perhaps not by virtue of him personally evangelising every member of that population, but because he has established key resource churches who by their very reproducing, planting and evangelising nature would see the work of the Great Commission completed throughout that whole region. An astonishing claim when the region covers from Jerusalem to Illyricum (Southern Yugoslavia or Albania).

Our churches and church plants need to be equipped, resourced and orientated towards the complete evangelisation of their whole area. Every house, work place, social sphere and stratum of society needs to be soaked and permeated with the good news of Jesus.

Our evangelism strategies need to be broad and all-embracing. Rather like the farmer in the parable of the sower (Mt 13:3–4), our activities will scatter the seed of the gospel over a wide terrain. We may have a specific focus from time to time, but basically our aim will be to see every individual, family and cultural grouping reached.

This kind of proclamation is ideally suited to the local body of Jesus, but is beyond the reach of the 'one hit', itinerant or crusade approach. The ongoing presence of the Christian church within the fabric of the community means that day by day we can be moving closer towards reaching people over and over again with the gospel. Time is on our side! How long this takes any church depends on the vibrancy, activity and resources of that church under God. Lawrence Singlehurst once suggested to me that in any case a church should have around a twenty-five-year vision to see its surrounding area fully permeated with Christians and the gospel.

My feeling is that this kind of continued evangelistic presence, as opposed to the yearly week-of-outreach model (because it is not happening during the other fifty-one weeks), will begin to see richer fruit.

I remember being interested when a friend of mine commented that the average person who comes to Christ does so after around seven encounters with the gospel. I was then astonished when another said that in Korea it was still after around six encounters! I sense that we often believe that in areas of revival the workings of God mean people just flock sovereignly into church and become Christians. This may well occur in some cases. However, if on average the church in Korea is reaching each convert six times before a decision is made, it means they do not just pray! They are a highly motivated, discipled and active church who are reaching phenomenal numbers of their population over and over again with the gospel. Maybe, if we had as healthy and committed a church as they, our results would be a little more similar to theirs!

An incarnation of the gospel

Churches also have a unique potential to encapsulate and express the gospel in a way that words or individuals cannot. We are in an age where words come particularly cheaply. People are suspicious of marketing techniques, media hype and verbal promises. They are looking for actions and often for the qualities of the gospel to be demonstrated before their eyes.

I remember one evening when a group of us from our church went out for a drink. One of our group brought a non-

Christian friend who was an active feminist and animal rights believer. Within minutes she was locked into an argument with one of our group! The words approach did not work! Not a good start for our witnessing – or so we thought. However, on the way home in the car she asked, "How do you become a Christian, and can I do it now?"

When asked why she wanted to, her reply was that she had watched people all evening. The love, intimate friendship and care within the group had impressed her deeply. The humour and jokes had been upbuilding and even the more lonely members of the group had been included and accepted. After seeing this she had concluded, "If this is Christianity, then I want in!"

As churches we are the body of Christ. We are called to 'flesh out' the life, character and qualities of our Head, that is Jesus. We do this together in a way that can never be achieved by individuals. We need every person, with his unique personality and giftings (1 Cor 12:14–20). There is a rich diversity within each member of the body, yet at the same time there is not an independence, but rather an interdependence. One is not complete without the other, and furthermore if we are to achieve the maturity and effectiveness to which we are called, we will need the breadth of all the ministries expressed in concert together (Eph 4:11–16).

Effective churches will be characterised by a corporate vision, goal and ethos; a people preoccupied with working together. Contending as one man for the gospel (Phil 1:27), their corporate expression will have an impact which seems disproportionately greater than the sum of the individual parts. It is this dynamic at work which I believe was one factor which caused the early church to "enjoy the favour of all the people" (Acts 2:47), thus resulting in daily additions to the church.

Prophetic activity

The church which impacts the community and learns to infiltrate new territory will be aware of its prophetic role in its area. This will be expressed at an individual and corporate level as the group proclaims and demonstrates the radical nature of the Christian worldview and lifestyle. We will need to turn ourselves inside out in order to be visible and available to all.

Our proclamation will hopefully reflect the life of the kingdom and by its very non-religious nature be an expression of real life in Jesus. It will reflect a concern for the community and reveal the heart of the church as a servant body in the area.

As a result, all our evangelism locally revolves around this model. In the context of our street work and door-to-door visitation, we will use community surveys which reveal the needs of the town and area, and we ask people how the church could serve them. This gives an opening for at least one further visit to share the survey's conclusions and the action we are taking.

We are also formulating evangelistic questionnaires focusing on green issues. These show the church's concern and ability to act, and also point the way to Creator God as the solution. Activities like March for Jesus give an opportunity for the church to gain profile and speak something positive, reflecting the good news, into the heart of our areas.

Our task is to gain a sufficiently distinct profile for all the people to be clear as to what we stand for and what the gospel is about.

Priestly activity

Our cutting edge in reaching people with the gospel for the first time will often be in the areas of kingdom justice and reconciliation. As each member of our communities brings his calling and commission to bear, our sphere of influence will enlarge. Some while ago, one of our leaders, Mike Morris, drew a team together to formulate a Christian Citizenship Charter. This would provide a framework for the church's activities in the community. During this process people have begun to catch the vision as to how they can change things.

Teams have cleared gardens, decorated rooms, cooked and shopped for the social services. ACET (Aids Care Education and Training) teams have given AIDS education in schools and home care in the community. A non-Christian friend told me how our church name and phone number are displayed prominently in her office at the hospital as a body which can supply help.

On top of this we have helped old people's homes, set up a chicken run, crop rotation and village shop for a children's home and also launched a major Romanian appeal. This appeal enlisted the help of local businesses and key figures to raise funding. We have sent three teams to Romania, refurbished orphanages and provided medical equipment. We have even persuaded the local ambulance chief to recondition an ambulance and send a team, led by one of our church members (an ambulance driver), to deliver it! Altogether well over £30,000 has been released, from non-Christian sources, into church projects there.

The cumulative community presence and profile gained from these types of activities is significant. People are more open to us in our direct evangelistic contacts because they have heard what we've been up to. Local politicians and dignitaries are also well-disposed to attending relevant evangelistic events as a result. Doors that would never normally be opened begin to invite access. For instance, during our Romanian appeal, the manager of the most prestigious department store in Chichester ran a fashion show for us at Goodwood House, the home of the Duchess of Richmond, who was the patron of our initiative. Subsequently he has opened his store to us, and we have used it for evangelistic meal events. Guests arrive for drinks, are given a tour of the store and then invited upstairs for a cabaret evening – a type of event that can be used to reach a section of our community which would be beyond the sphere of our normal evangelistic activity.

These examples serve to illustrate the need for the church to be present *in* the community. This is an aspect of spiritual warfare. On the one hand our worship, prayer and evangelism displace the spiritual forces that hold people in bondage (Eph 6:12), and on the other we move on and occupy the territory for Jesus because leaving a vacuum is dangerous (Mt 12:43–45).

We pray for those in social and spiritual bondage and provide practical avenues for their release. Only a people who live and breathe that town or village can adequately do this job. In my opinion, the preaching centre commuter model of church needs to be totally rethought. We are planting churches not meetings. Otherwise, the only time locals contact the so-called 'community church' is when its members roar into the area on a Sunday morning, waking everybody up and stealing their parking spaces!

Church planting involves a cost for all involved: teams moving house and often jobs; children moving schools. The impact of this on our communities will be significant. When the Cobham Fellowship planted in Tooting (London), twenty-six people moved from the leafy suburbs into a deprived inner-city area. A tremendous cost to the families was involved, affecting the schooling of their children, among many other things. The impact in Cobham was also significant. So many houses went on the market that a local estate agent complained that house prices would drop! The schools also said that their staffing levels would be affected due to the number of children leaving. In any case, within eighteen months that group had grown to over 100 people. Now, after three years, they number 150 and have planted one other congregation with yet more in the pipeline.

The scope for the church to express the gospel of the kingdom is endless. As we advance, our task is to cast the net of the kingdom (Mt 13:47–50) as broadly and as exhaustively as we can. The rest is up to Jesus.

Expressing community

Despite all this vast potential, we need to be clear that motivation and excitement alone will not produce what we are after. The heart, ethos and quality of our local churches will be the foundation upon which we will build. Our activities don't come from a hollow sense of duty, but flow from the abundant experience of God's love both as individuals and as a group.

People need to understand that in essence the church is

people and relationships and has nothing whatsoever to do with buildings. Our fellowship together will hopefully be real *koinonia*, a love, sharing and loyalty revealing a depth and quality almost akin to marriage. It is this context that provides the arena for discipleship and also for the healing which we all need as human beings.

I often feel that much of our counselling, inner healing and other pastoral activities would bear far more long-term fruit and even be unnecessary if people felt loved, cared for, identified with and significant within the community of the church. This is why I feel that as churches we have the potential to care far more adequately for the whole person than any secular body can.

Therefore time needs to be spent developing relationships and sharing together. Open hearts, families and marriages, along with a vulnerability and openness in friendship, must be our trademark. The richness and depth of our life together should bear the supernatural marks of fellowship in the Holy Spirit.

In this vein our family life will be somewhat different from that of non-Christians. I often feel that the church particularly misses out here. From my understanding, the Western nuclear family is not a model that appears biblically. Therefore many of our traditional 'husband, wife, 2.2 kids' family seminars are inadequate. The biblical pattern seems to be one of extended family or even the 'household' model. I have heard one commentator observe that some of these households could have numbered around 1,000 people, a mini village, including all the family members, slaves and whoever else happened to be around!

In consequence our church life will be a ferment of shared lives, homes and resources. We will live to give. Single people with resources will be pursuing shared accommodation, helping others with fewer means. Families will be making room to embrace single parents, homeless teenagers and others. Often, what is needed is not fundraising for a house project for the homeless, but a greater generosity and commitment for people in the church to open up their spare rooms and share their lives!

Shared lifestyles like this also have a profound impact evangelistically within our communities. We have a girl whose husband, also a Christian, left her and went off completely due to an adulterous relationship. She was pregnant and immediately a childless couple in the fellowship took her in. The wife was there throughout the birth, supporting the girl through it and through her subsequent divorce. The couple then sold their house and moved to a larger one with increased facilities to hold their larger family.

Now, a year on, mother and baby are well. Non-Christian friends at the mother and toddlers' group and other neighbours are confounded by this model of family. The girl's testimony has rung out and already around half a dozen people have come to Christ through it. There are other stories that could be told, but I hope the point is already clear: the quality of our church life, and our ability to encapsulate the values of the kingdom together, will have a direct bearing on the effectiveness of our churches, be they new churches or more established communities.

Cultural Relevance

Another great benefit in evangelising new areas through church planting is the fact that a culturally relevant community can be established. Often, in reaching into new areas, particularly housing estates, it can be difficult initially to integrate converts into the lifestyle of the home congregation. Its expression may be more suited to another age range or class make up. I will discuss this problem in greater depth later. However, for now, let us just say that a group which has been planted and contextualised within the new area has a greater chance of finding more relevant and effective evangelistic models, as well as expressing a community life to which others in the area will relate.

We prefer to operate as one church, covering the whole region with individual congregations working out the vision on the ground. Each congregation develops its own focus and flavour while remaining true to our distinctives and ethos as a whole church. That way we can enjoy the best of both worlds. The congregations infiltrate the different communities on the ground and enjoy the privilege of that. Then, when we meet together as a whole church on a monthly basis, we enjoy the fullness and riches of having a large gathering of all the different groups together. These are a fuller expression of the kingdom community which should prophetically display that the gospel breaks down all the barriers of race, sex, age and class (Eph 2:11–18; Gal 3:26–29).

Each time we have planted a congregation this benefit of cultural relevance has struck home. More recently we have established new work in the Bersted area of Bognor Regis. The initial six months were spent surveying the area, meeting people, frequenting the community centre (the local pub), taking part in their quizzes, having pub house groups and even staging our own Karaoke event there. As a result, a few converts appeared and we planned a major community kids' playscheme in the summer – an event, that through our surveys, we were sure met the main needs of that area.

During that week we had over 100 kids daily, signed up nearly sixty for a new kids' club and saw fourteen teenagers and around half a dozen adults converted. There were also well over 100 warm contacts to follow up. At the focal point of the week we had a family fun day. There were never less than 500 people there and we believe around 1,000 people attended. Of these, 95% travelled on foot to the event. All these people in the area have now heard of us as a church and know a little of what we are about.

A good start for a new congregation! Our programme had been funded partially by the social services. The worker who visited us was surprised that anybody would want to do an event in Bersted. At the end of the week, seeing its success, he commented to James Sharp, one of the congregational leaders, "Now I know why you've started a new church here. Without the church you couldn't run the event or draw the community in. With the church you can serve the community in this way."

Not a bad grasp of our ethos for a non-Christian!

Change or bust

Obviously for the church to develop, grow and plant in all these spheres we are looking for growth at every level: in numbers, maturity, quality and conceptual understanding; in resources and giving as well as in breadth and depth. I see no reason why this shouldn't be our normative expectation, as it is my firm belief that growth is the normal and natural state for any believer and church to be in. If growth is not being experienced, be sure that something is wrong or lacking.

One thing is sure: a major feature in any growing community needs to be the ability to be flexible and prosper in an atmosphere of rapid change. Many churches do not grow because of a weakness here. They have static concepts relating to leadership, meetings and church structure. New things are generally resisted and need to be slipped in by leaders with kid gloves on.

I believe flexibility has nothing to do with age. Some students I have met are the most boring, inflexible lot possible, while some of our senior citizens are the most radical. Flexibility has to do with how we have been birthed and discipled in God and whether we have the right foundations in our lives.

Our new churches need to reflect flexible foundations. People need to be seeking change and desiring new things from God. Our leaders need to be developing and moving on to new things, creating room for others to come through. In this environment, constant change will seem normal, be it changes in vision, new initiatives, the cancellation of others and the general mêlée that always accompanies the moving of the Spirit. Change becomes the air in which we breath. People's security is firmly in God and in their relationships rather than in the static nature of their church life.

In this context, people's vision and goals need to remain firmly focused on Jesus. He is our focal point, the King whose kingdom we seek above all things. As churches, we must avoid at all costs being building, plant or project orientated. Such things form the scaffolding around which we build, but are poor substitutes for a real expression of church life. Our church's life will be organic, spontaneous and life-centred, while at the same time having a clear structure, strategy, order and pattern.

Retaining this balance will keep us on course and enable us to reproduce after our own at every level. In this state we will be continually planting and have a rich people resource continually moving forward into fresh realms of leadership.

As leaders, our main task will then be to keep on our toes and effectively channel all this potential!

CHAPTER 7

THE PROCESS OF EARLY CHURCH PLANTING

Acts 16 presents us with a wonderfully illuminating view of the process of early church planting. The people involved, the strategies followed, the spiritual battles fought and the breakthroughs achieved all unfold before our eyes. Over the years it has proved a seminal passage of Scripture for me, and we are going to examine it closely at this point to see how it confirms the view of church planting we are presenting in this book. The chapter falls neatly into four sections: people, strategy, battle and breakthrough.

People (Acts 16:1–4)

On coming to Lystra, Paul met up with Timothy, whom he wanted to join his team (v3). Team is fundamental to church planting, because we cannot plant church if we don't have the seed of church already present. Church is corporate, so the embryonic church already needs to exist among the people who are planting it. This is a major problem for us today in societies where satanic strongholds have destroyed or damaged the institutions of family, society and even church itself. As a result, many of us find it hard to build trusting relationships. Of course this is more or less true in all societies and is precisely the reason why new churches need to be planted where these trusting relationships can be established and past hurts and damage repaired.

It is encouraging to realise that the context of Paul's team building at this point was the earlier breakdown of team in his relationships with Barnabas and John Mark. This is because the situation (which seems to have been at least partially restored later – cf 2 Tim 4:11) did not make Paul give up on team life; neither should we.

It is important to realise, however, that Paul seems to have chosen Timothy very carefully. He had his own spiritual history and background which made him suitable for the task. His mother was a Jewish believer, and Paul's later letter to him makes clear that his grandmother was too and that this heritage had produced "sincere faith" in Timothy (2 Tim. 1:5). His father was not a believer, and was a Greek, which meant that Timothy's faith had been well tested and that he understood the context of the Greek-influenced cultures into which Paul was travelling. Then there was the already quite widespread all-round reputation that Timothy had established. Church-planting teams begin as small groups, but they need to have the potential to be the foundation of a large work, so the spiritual history of those who are part of it needs to be well developed. Furthermore Timothy demonstrated an astonishing degree of commitment both to Paul and to the cross-cultural sensitivities of those among whom he was likely to be working. Paul wanted this man to go with him; and he took him and circumcised him because of the Jews who were in those parts (v3).

Those of us who are familiar with Bible language can read statements like this almost without noticing. But I suspect that if Roger Forster, my team leader, had suggested he circumcise me before I joined his team back in 1974 I would have felt it as something of a shock to the system! It is reputed to be among the most painful physical operations an adult male can experience, quite apart from the intensely personal nature of the act! But church planting across cultures, breaking barriers of race, sex and social background is a calling that requires a readiness to experience intense pain and extraordinary personal vulnerability. The level of commitment required means a preparedness for the flesh to be circumcised, not literally but spiritually: namely, death to our own personal likes and dislikes, dispositions, attitudes and cultural identities wherever they stand in the way of the kingdom of God. Paul's words to the Colossians make clear that Jesus is "the head over all rule and authority" and "in Him you were also circumcised with a circumcision made without hands, in the removal of the body of the flesh by the circumcision of Christ" (Col 2:10–11). Church planters need to be living in the good of this.

The final point to emphasise about church planting people here, is the level of loyalty they gave to the decisions of the apostles and elders in Jerusalem. "Now while they were passing through the cities, they were delivering the decrees, which had been decided upon by the apostles and elders who were in Jerusalem, for them to observe. So the churches were being strengthened in the faith, and were increasing in number daily" (Acts 16: v 4–5).

Paul's later writings make it quite clear that he had serious reservations about the importance of some of the contents of these decrees. The decrees were "that they abstain from things contaminated by idols and from fornication and from what is strangled and from blood" (Acts 15:20). Whereas Paul never shifted his ground over fornication, which is securely fixed by Jesus' own teaching (cf Mt 5:27–28, 32), Paul did eventually take a much weaker view on the other items (cf Rom 14:14). Despite his reservations, Paul and his team were loyal to the Jerusalem leaders. This pragmatic approach to some of the controversial non-essentials of theology both guards the faith and avoids the unnecessary disagreements which can destroy teams and the churches they set out to plant. Instead, this loyal pragmatism produces strengths and increase. We have a lot to learn from it.

Strategy (Acts 16:6–15)

Paul's strategy strikes a delightful balance between the supernatural and the natural. So often we tend to emphasise one or the other. But here both the prophetic word and the background administrative skill are clearly at work. We need both those who are sure they know what needs to be done as well as those who can work out how we are going to do it. One may appear supernatural and the other natural. Both can be equally spiritual. In this piece of early church planting process the strategy was decided supernaturally in at least two ways: through what appear to be examples of prophetic words– either direct prophecy or the application of supernaturally given wisdom – and through a supernatural vision. "They passed through the Phrygian and Galatian region, having been forbidden by the Holy Spirit to speak the word in Asia" (v6) and "they were trying to go into Bithynia, and the Spirit of Jesus did not permit them" (v7).

I have wondered whether the use of different words to describe the Holy Spirit's activity in directing their strategy here suggests the use of more than one prophetic gift, such as a word of prophecy and a word of wisdom. But it cannot be proved conclusively from the text. What we can say is that at least one prophetic gift must have been used on this occasion to conclude that it was the Holy Spirit stopping them, not the devil or merely the practical difficulties of the route. The vision is unequivocal. This was a supernatural manifestation that brought precise revelation from the Holy Spirit as to the way ahead.

What is clear from all this is that church-planting strategy needs to be formulated in an atmosphere of the Holy Spirit's presence and the manifestation of Holy Spirit gifts, otherwise the supernatural guidance will be missed. Once again the easiest way to ensure that we follow this kind of strategy is to give adequate time for worship in the Holy Spirit (cf Eph. 5:18–19) in order that the gifts have opportunity to operate. That this was early church-planting practice is obvious from Paul's original commission to leave Antioch with Barnabas (Acts 13:1–2) and from their response to the gross physical persecution after their imprisonment in Philippi in the chapter we are currently exploring (v25).

In our own contemporary experience of church planting in the Ichthus Fellowship we have experienced definite supernatural guidance in this way. Several years ago we had a small team of folk eager to plant out in Beckenham, a rather more comfortable suburb than many of our priority targets. However, they felt there was a real need there, so after some months of prayer and contact-making we planned a barbeque at the house of one of the team member's. Nobody came! To make up for it we set ourselves to worship and pray. After a while an older lady in the group interrupted. "I think I've got it," she said. "If the gospel is good news to the poor and that's our strategy, we should focus on the poorer parts of the suburb." We all recognised the voice of the Holy Spirit and soon identified the Churchfields end of Beckenham as the place to start. Since then a thriving church has been planted which has in turn planted out several more. Similarly our strategy for the Middle East was powerfully shaped when one of our leadership team had a dream in which he was directed to Cyprus where we now have a growing cross-cultural church from which further church planting and training is proceeding. However, despite the clear supernatural guidance, these experiences did not bring churches into being alone. An enormous amount of practical work was also needed. And this was clearly the case in the Early Church experience of Paul and his team. Once the man from Macedonia had appeared to him in the night-time vision they immediately "sought to go into Macedonia, concluding that God had called us to preach the gospel to them"(v10). The following verses imply an extraordinary amount of hidden practical administrative activity. "Putting out to sea", "ran a straight course", "on the day following", (v11) "from there to Philippi which is a leading city of the district of Macedonia ... a Roman colony", "staying in this city for some days"(v12). and "where we supposed that there would be a place of prayer" (v13) imply hiring boats, engaging mariners, consulting timetables and employing navigational skills, and geographical and sociological research. We have found the background skills to be equally but not more important than the seemingly more remarkable spiritual gifts. All combine together in the work of church planting. We have found the work of researching the social, geographical and historical background of an area especially important. When it is not done we will fail to be at the right place at the right time to meet the people God has in view. The operation of the Holy Spirit is vital at all times, as it was with Lydia when "the Lord opened her heart to respond to the things spoken by Paul" (v14). But the practical observation and sharing of past experience and expertise led them to the riverside in the first place, where they met Lydia and the other praying women.

It is important to guard carefully both these aspects of strategy. Sometimes we think we know all about a place, its people and its needs. Especially if we live there. Some years ago I was invited to lead a practical weekend in evangelism at a church plant in a South Coast town. The church was being planted in a community centre on a middle-income housing estate where most of the leadership team were living. While explaining Jesus' strategy to the poor, I asked whether there were any council tenants or immigrant communities represented, as they often fall into that category. I was assured that there were none. Hardly had we left the community centre for some practical research work when I saw an African girl coming out of a shop. A few minutes later we also identified a small block of council flats and later an Asian family in real social need. This kind of work is essential if we too are going to be in partnership with the Holy Spirit in a supernatural way. Research of this kind involves both simple practical observation and networking, but can also involve consulting libraries and local government records. Local census records are readily publicly available in the UK.

In the end, of course, no strategy either supernaturally or practically formulated and carried out will be complete without experimental action, namely doing some evangelism! Luke encompasses a whole range of emotions and risks in the simple words "we sat down and began speaking to the women" (v13). Without that practical bold experiment there would have been no success. So it is still!

Battle (Acts 16:16–24)

The multiplication and consolidation of the Philippian church happened through experiences of demonic confrontation followed by extreme persecution and subsequent supernatural deliverance. It is my conviction that a spiritual battle was taking place along the same lines as Jesus himself experienced and that it provides us with important guidelines and insights for all church-planting situations. Many churches flounder and stagnate after the initial successful stages of church planting. The Lydias and their households are won and discipled. But then the problems begin. In fact many churches have simply institutionalised and preserved this early experience of opposition and remain more or less stuck for a whole generation or more.

If I am right, this chapter provides a helpful diagnosis for many church situations, and can provide us with applied principles for spiritual warfare and breakthrough today. Paul and his team established the first stage of church planting with the conversion of Lydia and her household. This was not a small thing, for in those days a merchant in the Roman empire might well have a household of a hundred or more people, and it is clear that a significant number had joined the church as Paul and his team are described as visiting "the brethren" in Lydia's house before they move on to Thessalonica (v40). As they worked on building up the church in Lydia's house and continued to pray together with the women by the river, they were confronted for many days by a demonised girl.

It is clear from the subsequent events that she represented the satanic strongholds of the city. She brought "her masters much profit by fortunetelling" (v16). These masters had extraordinary power in the city and were not only able to stir up the crowds, but also had great influence with the magistrates who, contrary to Roman law, themselves "tore their robes off them and proceeded to order them to be beaten with rods" (v22). As we have already seen in the earlier chapter on spiritual warfare, Jesus' church planting is an attack on the strongholds of Satan on the earth. Once a church begins to be planted then it begins to engage those strongholds. We have seen how Jesus and his disciples did it, so it is not at all surprising to find it happening again here. Strongholds of materialism and power had provided a way for occultism and the exploitation of the weak. As the church was planted and began to grow it was inevitable that these powers would be encountered.

It is significant in this connection that the demons recognised the contrary spiritual authority of the apostolic team. "Following after Paul and us, she kept crying out, saying, 'These men are bond-servants of the Most High God, who are proclaiming to you the way of salvation'" (v17). Notice that Paul did not let the devil set the agenda for him, but continued to the place of prayer for many days before finally dealing with the evil spirit.

It is worth noting here that Jesus gave some definite guidelines about this kind of encounter, which it is safe to assume that Paul and his team were following. When the disciples failed to cast out the demon from the boy after the transfiguration, Jesus explained, "This kind cannot come out by anything but prayer" (Mk 9:29). Many manuscripts add "and fasting". Jesus also made it clear that "no one can enter the strong man's house... unless he first binds the strong man, and then he will plunder his house" (Mk 3:27). Jesus was praying and fasting and resisting Satan in the wilderness before ever he cast out specific demons.

The implication is that Paul and his team bound the devil in his particular expression or stronghold during those many prayer times, before he cast the demon from the girl. However, the initial success was then massively resisted by the enemy. Some people ask how this can be if the enemy was fully bound. The answer is that he wasn't; he was bound in connection with his hold on the girl. This is in full accord with Jesus' own experience where he resisted and partly bound Satan in the wilderness at his temptations, but even Jesus' power did not bind him and cast him out finally until the cross. And as we have already considered elsewhere, although his final defeat is secured it still has to be appropriated and enforced by the saints of God in the earth (cf Rev 12:10–11). Once the girl was dealt with and delivered, the enemy stronghold in the place was drawn out, exposed and uncovered.

This was a very difficult time, but the team seemed to understand what was going on and knew what to do. Paul shows extraordinary foresight and courage. Had he revealed his Roman citizenship – produced his passport, so to speak – at the beginning of the trouble they would surely have been spared the persecution. But spiritual warfare has to be fought with spiritual weapons. So, like Jesus, they were prepared to lay down their lives, and also like him they knew the power of prayer and praise. So having been violently abused and beaten, secured in the inner prison with their feet shackled in the stocks "Paul and Silas were praying and singing hymns of praise to God". This spiritual warfare was remarkably successful! And God released the same resurrection power that Jesus had pioneered and secured for them in Jerusalem at the cross. An earthquake opened the prison, just as it had opened his tomb (Mt 28:2). The jailer and his household were converted and the church successfully and publicly established and recognised, just as 3000 were added and the church publicly established at Pentecost.

Breakthrough (Acts 16:25–40)

This is the breakthrough that we need to experience in so many church planting situations today. We have had some encouraging beginnings of this kind of breakthrough in our church planting experience in Ichthus, but we need to get right through into our own version of Pentecost. This is surely what Jesus secured for us in his death and resurrection. "When he had disarmed the rulers and authorities, he made a public display of them, having triumphed over them through him" (Col 2:15).

In our many different church planting situations we have had almost countless embryonic versions of the process. Most of them are difficult to cite because they are either still in process or involve obviously identifiable personalities. We can tell the whole story, hopefully, at some future time. However I believe it is necessary to give a contemporary concrete example of this process, so with some hesitancy I cite the experience of a Kent church I was involved in as a student some 25 years ago. It is significant as it was one of the first new churches founded in the current Charismatic move of the Spirit. After the initial years of planting, growth and spiritual life the fellowship was overtaken by what, with hindsight, can best be described as a spirit of slander which directly attacked individual leaders and set them against each other. The effects were disastrous and the church was effectively destroyed. Those pioneers were, I think, encountering ancient strongholds of religious power and position which were long established in that vicinity of Kent because of the proximity of the city of Canterbury.

It is intriguing and exciting to record that last year an unofficial but interdenominational group of church leaders met in the area and together agreed to repent on behalf of those who gave place to that spiritual attack all those years ago, and a representative of those attacked and undermined forgave them. Within weeks one of our Ichthus new church plants in the area experienced the beginnings of a now almost total reversal of slanderous attacks from inside and outside the fellowship, and previously devastated relationships began to be restored! We need much more revelation and obedience to the Holy Spirit in these matters.Then the revival we are looking for will stop eluding us.

Here in the Book of Acts the spiritual attack came from outside the church. In the example I gave of the Kent church the attacks penetrated to the inside. These are more painful to deal with, but are possible to repulse because they are the kind Jesus and his team experienced. However difficult the situations may be, it is always possible to work them out if we follow the principles of church discipline outlined by Jesus in passages like Matthew 18, which we will consider in detail later. The crucial point is to recognise the context of spiritual battle as Jesus so clearly did in the example of Judas Iscariot.

In his case one of the team, described by Peter as "numbered among us, and allotted his share in this ministry" (Acts 1:17, RSV) had been subverted by Satan. The chief priest and leaders of the Jews had formed a power group susceptible to money which had become a stronghold for the devil. It was this stronghold that drew Judas through his own sin and openness to Satan.

John 13 shows how Jesus dealt with this desperate situation threatening the embryonic church. As John described it:

> And during supper, the devil having already put into the heart of Judas Iscariot, the son of Simon, to betray Him, Jesus, knowing that the Father had given all things into His hands, and that He had come forth from God, and was going back to God, rose from supper, and laid aside His garments; and taking a towel ... began to wash the disciples' feet (Jn 13:2–5).

The clue to giving a positive lead in this kind of battle as well as worship (Jn 13:31; cf Mt 26:3) is to know who we are in terms of spiritual history and destiny (Jn 13:3), to go on lovingly serving both friends and betrayers (13:5), to be prepared to be vulnerable to our potential betrayer in order to give something of God to them (13:26), to renew our fundamental vows of love (13:34) and to lay down our lives as Jesus did! Resurrection followed Jesus, and the foundation of the church was secured for ever.

Paul knew all about this kind of leading when he wrote to the Romans: "As it is written, 'For Thy sake we are being put to death all day long'" (Rom 8:36). It was this extraordinary readiness of Paul's to die, literally if necessary, that was the key to breakthrough in Philippi.

As we have seen, he could have produced his Roman citizenship at any time in the persecution experience. Instead he relied on spiritual weapons. Then when the breakthrough was achieved, he consolidated it. His spiritual authority over the enemy's strongholds was first in prayer and worship and the laid down life, then and only then was there a place for social, political or legal action. This secured the church as a stronghold of God in Macedonia for the future.

> Now when day came, the chief magistrates sent their policemen, saying, 'Release those men.' And the jailer reported these words to Paul, saying, 'The chief magistrates have sent to release you. Now therefore come out and go in peace.' But Paul said to them, 'They have beaten us in public without trial, men who are Romans and have thrown us into prison; and now are they sending us away secretly? No indeed! But let them come themselves and bring us out ' (v35–37).

The magistrates were obliged to come and appeal to them, and so the apostolic team's authority was recognised and established by the local magistrates. Even though the magistrates begged them to leave, Paul and the team still took their own time to visit and encourage the church. In this way the church was fully planted.

Once again this opportunity to consolidate publicly the stronghold of God has been something we have experienced after spiritual battles, both with our own local civic authorities here in London and also in the tougher political situations of the Middle East.

CHAPTER 8

MODELS OF MINISTRY

It has often been stressed that church structures in and of themselves do not create growth. However, they can certainly inhibit it. Structures are merely the wineskin, the container, while only God himself can provide the new wine of his Holy Spirit. In addition to this, I believe that our attitude to the gifts and ministries of the Holy Spirit can either restrict growth or release it significantly into the life of the church. Churches that have either a completely or partially dispensationalist attitude to these gifts and ministries are cutting God's supply lines of life and growth which serve to exhort, encourage and mature the body of Christ (Eph 4:11–16). Certainly without an apostolic or prophetic dimension our planting will lack the basic foundations upon which we can build and reproduce (Eph 2:20).

In this chapter I want to examine briefly some of the apparent distinctives within the church leadership and ministry of the New Testament. In doing this we will hopefully be able to adjust models where necessary and also, where appropriate, embrace new modes of operation.

This exercise is particularly important because so many churches are bound by their patterns of ministry, and to reproduce these patterns through the process of church planting will only perpetuate their problems rather than create a body of believers which has the necessary foundations to implement a Great Commission style vision.

New Testament patterns

One of the first things we notice as we look into the New Testament is the flexibility and dynamic nature of the church as it grew under God's hand from its humble beginnings in the Upper Room. People's understanding of church evolved with their growth as their structures broadened (Acts 6:1-7). Into this mix comes the teaching on leadership and church given by Jesus and within the pastoral epistles.

Here it appears that we are not given a blueprint that is to apply at all times and in all places, but rather biblical principles of leadership and ministry that can be applied and reapplied as we grow and seek to relate within different cultures and in different generations.

For instance, it is clear that initially the early Jewish Christian communities drew their ecclesiology from the Synagogue. Their eldership structure, meeting style and worship expressions would have reflected this. It was only as the gospel began to take root within the Gentile population that further expressions of church life and practice emerged. Initially, these changes were resisted by some in the Jewish congregations. This resistance was mainly over the law, but no doubt also stemmed from racism and the difficulty of grasping change. However, it was clear from an early stage that change would occur, and as it was accepted and absorbed, the church continued to grow (Acts 15:1–29).

Within church planting, change, adaptability to new cultural settings and the development of relevant leadership models are crucial. In this dynamic development it is more important that we retain the key elements and function of church leadership than it is to have the right title for it. For instance, to my mind the word 'elder' has no meaning within the culture that our church operates. It conjures up weird notions in people's minds. Therefore, we would not use it, preferring the term 'congregational leader' for our local leadership. This term is accessible to the non-Christians around us in the way that 'elder' would have been to the first-century Jewish converts.

However, although we have dispensed with the name, the biblical function and qualifications remain clearly in place and are readily applied to our congregational leadership.

In addition, I believe that historically many denominations have created problems for themselves by using the word 'pastor' as the title for their local church leader. In Ephesians 4:11 this ministry appears and the Greek word is *poimen* which means 'to shepherd', clearly drawing the analogy of the shepherd's care of the flock with a caring ministry within the church (eg Acts 20:28; Jn 10). This term denotes the ministry and action of shepherding rather than referring to an office of local church leadership. Furthermore, when referring to the office of local church leadership, *poimen* is not used but rather the words *episkopos* (overseer, bishop) or *presbuteros* (elder) are employed. We will draw some of the functions of church leadership from the words later. However, the use of the term 'pastor', and the exclusive identification of it with the local leader, has meant that in many cases evangelistic, prophetic and apostolic giftings have been pushed out of local leadership as an exclusively pastoral/maintenance emphasis is pursued.

This has resulted in a lopsided, safe church leadership which often lacks a cutting edge and the ability to evangelise effectively. As a result, the evangelist is often driven out of the local church and dwells in the domain of the big crusade or the para-church organisation.

Alternatively, an evangelist may be subjected to many years' frustration in local church leadership trying to function as the pastor, feeling like a square peg in a round hole. Some of the clear observable features of the New Testament church will help us to avoid these common pitfalls.

Plurality of leadership

First, in New Testament terms there is no such thing as one man or one woman ministry. Local leadership is always in a team (Acts 20:28; Phil 1:1), and the work of establishing a new church was not considered over until a group of elders had been installed (Tit 1:5). There are many churches which have been in existence for years yet are without a team leadership and so are not yet firmly established under these criteria. The benefits of multi-gifted team ministry are obvious and the church without it will always struggle to reproduce and advance on a broad front.

A leader of leaders

Within this plurality of leadership and shared team responsibility it is clear that there was mutual submission (Eph 5:21); a learning from and deferring to one another's differing gifts and perspectives. However, to retain impetus and clarity it seems that normally each church would have a leader of leaders. It appears that James assumed this role in the Jerusalem church as people deferred to him to find a solution to the controversy over the law and the Gentile Christians (Acts 15:1–29).

On many occasions I have encountered churches that try to operate with no leader of leaders, insisting that the Holy Spirit leads. This often leaves those with the visionary gifts paralysed at the mercy of non-visionaries, or disillusioned, thus producing a church that has no distinct vision or thrust and that spins around in circles.

The leader of leaders should provide the context for the rest of the team to operate and use their individual gifts. He or she will normally be equipped with visionary abilities and will also be able to incorporate and yield to the perspectives and vision of the wider team, while at the same time keeping things moving forward.

The Holy Spirit leads the church through dynamically gifted individuals who then express their diversity in team. Some people's character and gifts work best within the overall context of a team, while others naturally operate in the team leadership role.

Complementary gifts

While there are certain key functions that the local team of leaders need to cover as part of their 'office', the group of leaders needs to reflect a good mix of the ministries and giftings. It is not too important whether or not team leaders are pastoral, evangelistic or multi-gifted, provided they are able to make room for the rest of the team to function. However, in a church-planting situation particularly, this main leader needs to be what we call a 'breakthrough person'. That is, someone who can carry the vision, motivate and exort the people and has a natural pioneering cutting edge to their abilities which will lead the new church in unity to impact its area.

I have observed several church plants which while having a good, strong, broad based leadership, have lacked a person with 'breakthrough' qualities and have therefore progressed very slowly, if at all.

The balance of giftings is key to the success of any church leadership. Rather than labelling the apostolic, prophetic and evangelistic ministries 'growth', and the pastoral ministries 'maintenance', I see that all ministry is growth ministry. As it was once commented, perhaps the evangelist gets the person out of Egypt and the pastor gets Egypt out of the person!

Furthermore, I believe that Scripture demands that the evangelist has a pastoral heart and vice versa. In church planting the pastor will have ample opportunity to do the work of the evangelist while the evangelists begin to realise the consequences of their activity and learn to be part of the establishing of successful pastoral and nurturing structures which hold the new converts.

It may well be that limited people resources mean that for a while we have a gift mix that is too narrow. This may not indicate a lack of gifted people; but it may mean that these folk are as yet too immature character wise for leadership. In this situation the plant may need outside input from a person who can help them to cover this area. Within our church it has been inappropriate for us to bring our key evangelist into local leadership because of his wider travelling commitments.

However, all of our congregations use him regularly on both a consultancy and ministry basis. This has released considerable fruit into the church and has given us time to develop our emerging ministries without giving them leadership too early.

The functions of local leadership

As we move on to summarise some of the functions of local leadership, it is worth noting again the whole basis upon which biblical leadership operates; that is, out of servanthood (Mt 20:25–28; 1 Pet 5:1–6). Leadership involves initiative and at times the exertion of authority, particularly in areas of church discipline (1 Cor 5:1–3; 2 Cor 2:5–11). However, as Christians we do not operate out of status, pulling rank in some kind of promotion ladder. Generally, the operation of our leadership will involve plainly setting forth the word of God (2 Cor 4:2) to a people who are open to persuasion and wanting to respond to God (Heb 13:7). Often society threatens to mould us into more status and authority orientated leadership, but we must be clear, making sure that our leadership models are firmly based on the example of Jesus. As Steve Clifford once observed, "Leadership is a serving relationship which has the effect of facilitating human development." Servanthood is therefore the A – Z of leadership.

As discussed earlier, the two words used to describe the local church leadership are *episkopos* (translated 'overseer' or 'bishop') and *presbuteros* (elder). These words are apparently used interchangeably to describe the same area of leadership. The word 'oversight' aptly describes the function of local leadership and occurs a number of times, particularly in the Septuagint, and describes the activities of watching over (Deut 11:12), leading out and bringing direction (Num 27:17).

Elsewhere, leadership is seen as:

Overseeing initiation and entrance into the community (Prov 3:23 – elders control the gates to the city; Jn 10:16 – shepherds the gate to the sheep).

Maintaining doctrinal and moral purity as well as church discipline (Mt 18:15–19; 1 Cor 5:3, 13; Tit 1:10–11).

Regulating who speaks publicly (Acts 13:15).

Standing at the head of the community giving direction (1 Tim 5:17; 1 Thess 5:12–13 – the word *proistemi*, ruling).

Leading, guiding and governing (Heb 13:7,17 – *hegeomai*).

The operation of godly leadership will require a delicate balance between the exercise of initiative, the maintenance of order (1 Cor 14:40) and the activity of serving and releasing others to express freely the workings of the Holy Spirit in their lives.

Where there is a vacuum of leadership, any growth will be unstable, volatile and can be lost as quickly as it has been gained. By contrast, a leadership that insists on tying up all the loose ends and eradicating all grey areas is in danger of organising the Holy Spirit out of a job. As a friend of mine once commented, 'If you want to find predictable order in church, go to the graveyard. There you'll find the graves all neatly in lines!' Death is often orderly. Life, however, has the alarming tendency to be spontaneous, disorderly, chaotic and full of surprises!

The Apostolic Dimension

I have already mentioned how important I view the role of apostolic ministry in the pioneering and development of new churches. There is no room here for a detailed study of this issue. However, I would like to make some preliminary observations and apply these specifically to the whole area of church planting.

Those who hold a dispensationalist approach to the gifts and ministries of the Holy Spirit like to restrict the experience of these phenomena to the confines of the early church. The growth of the renewal movement has meant that many have begun to embrace the 1 Corinthians 12 and Romans 12 gifts and ministries, even recognising the teacher, pastor, evangelist and prophet from Ephesians 4. However, in all but a very few areas, this has stopped short of the release of apostolic ministry.

Ephesians 4:11–16 reveals to us how key this ministry is in the maturing and development of the whole church:

It was he who gave some to be apostles, some to be prophets, some to be evangelists, and some to be pastors and teachers, to prepare God's people for works of service, so that the body of Christ may be built up until we all reach unity in the faith and in the knowledge of the Son of God and become mature, attaining to the whole measure of the fulness of Christ.

Then we will no longer be infants, tossed back and forth by the waves, and blown here and there by every wind of teaching and by the cunning and craftiness of men in their deceitful scheming. Instead, speaking the truth in love, we will in all things grow up into him who is the Head, that is, Christ. From him the whole body, joined and held together by every supporting ligament, grows and builds itself up in love, as each part does its work.

In embracing the apostolic we are by no means elevating today's apostles to the same level as the original twelve. These were perhaps chosen by Jesus to correspond to the twelve patriarchs and model prophetically the New Israel (Gal 6:16) that he was drawing together in the church. These individuals witnessed Jesus' life, death and resurrection, and as such were able to pen the unchanging truth of the New Testament canon and establish the core 'apostolic doctrine'.

However, elsewhere Scripture reveals to us that others were called apostles (Acts 14:14; Rom 16:7), travelled with Paul on his apostolic team and clearly exercised an apostolic function in the churches (1 Cor 3:5; 4:15). Just as the evangelist has a key ministry in reaching the unbeliever, so we will see that the apostle has an irreplaceable role in the ongoing development and establishing of churches. Furthermore, it seems strange that while only one person in the New Testament is called an evangelist (Acts 21:8), many more are designated apostles. Today we have many recognised evangelists, but few acknowledged apostles. In the light of this, the neglect of the apostolic would appear to be a major contemporary ecclesiological oversight!

Apostolic functions [1]

In trying to draw an understanding of the apostolic, there are a number of dangers that face us. First, there is the thinking that sees Paul as the stereotype of the apostle. While much of our thinking on the subject needs to be drawn from his incredible life and ministry, if it is only those who match him who have made the grade then no wonder there are not many contemporary examples!

Secondly, we can make an equal and opposite error. That is to see anyone who operates extra-locally as an apostle. We need to understand that we are talking about a distinct gifting from God rather than a 'successful pastor' who begins to operate his ministry in a wider sphere.

Thirdly, we need to avoid establishing a static blueprint of church structure which, while attempting to restore the Ephesians 4 ministries, introduces a static pyramid structure incorporating a kind of extra-local 'apostolic pope'. Again I refer to an observation made earlier in this chapter: that is, how flexible, adaptable and dynamic the early church structures appeared to be. Far from encountering a structural strait-jacket, we have key ministries and core truths that will be expressed in different ways depending on the cultural context and other mitigating factors.

Sent and Released

The basic meaning of the word 'apostle' is 'sent one' (Acts 13:1–3). As such, he or she (Rom 17:7 – Junias, is a woman's name) will have a commission and calling from the Holy Spirit which will be recognised and released by the leaders in the church, particularly other apostles.

When this has occurred they will begin to carry out their ministry in other geographical locations, while clearly retaining their accountability to the 'mother' church. It is worth noting that after his missionary journeys Paul would report back to Antioch (Acts 14:21–28) and even after his disagreement and subsequent parting of ways with Barnabas, Paul resubmitted himself to the Antioch leadership and was again commissioned to travel, this time with Silas (Acts 15 36–41).

It is also worth noting that the concept of team, so endemic to Jesus' discipleship model (Lk 10:1–2; 17) and the local church, is also a key to the function of the apostles. Paul particularly travelled in groups of two to three upwards. In fact, it is possible to count up to twenty-seven different people who travelled with him at one time or another. These teams would consist of the main leader (a Paul), some complementary ministries and personalities (a Barnabas) and also individuals who were in training for key areas of leadership (a Timothy). One wonders how much more effective all extra-local ministry would be if it could learn to operate in this manner.

Foundations

Because apostles are included in the Ephesians 4 ministries, it is vital that they are recognised and received in order that churches may be developed and grow to maturity (Eph 4:13). In fact, it could be said that the ministries in this passage together describe the apostle's function. Rather than being specialists, apostles will normally have the ability to operate broadly across these ministry areas and as such are uniquely equipped to lay balanced and secure foundations in leadership and church life. This ability may well elude the person who is strongly and specifically gifted in one particular area. We have already identified some of the drawbacks within an over-emphasis on the pastoral ministry. It is also fair to say that an overdose of the teaching, prophetic or evangelistic ministries will also reproduce deficiencies in one area or another.

While there are those who are specifically gifted as apostles, I believe that the other ministries are able to carry out apostolic work extra-locally when given a context and operating in team with an apostle.

With this in mind, it is not surprising how important the development, release and recognition of apostolic ministry is within our church planting. Local elders in isolation will not be able to plant the kind of churches that will grow, develop and themselves reproduce.

In Corinth Paul referred to his ministry as that of a wise master builder (1 Cor 3:10), providing the groundwork onto which others can build. In the planting of churches, it is those with apostolic gifting who will normally have a visionary instinct for the strategy and location of new churches. They will then quickly establish the necessary foundations, identifying other key people who will be able to build on an ongoing basis into the church. In this respect, it is clear that in New Testament times they had an involvement in the development of leadership in its early stages and also in the appointment of eldership (Tit 1:5) and ongoing nurturing of the churches (2 Cor 11:28).

It seems that apostles (like those with other ministries) have a God-given sphere of operation (2 Cor 10:12–16). This may change as time goes on, but will usually involve them predominantly in the activity of church planting. However, there may well be existing churches which do not have access to apostolic ministry. These may invite others to come and serve them in this area. The apostolic team then comes to serve the local eldership and their respective spheres dovetail together for the benefit of the whole body. Usually the local church very soon experiences a wider vision, a consolidation of their foundations and a release of ministry to reflect their particular needs. Often the apostle is able to release this in ways that local eldership cannot.

As apostles serve the local church and their ministry is confirmed by its fruit (1 Cor 9:2), often the local body can have the privilege and opportunity to facilitate a wider vision. This may happen through financial support of the apostle's ministry (Acts 4:35; 1 Cor 9:1–14), other churches that he or she is linked to (2 Cor 8–9), or the release of key emerging ministry to help in the wider work and to be trained in that context.

It is obvious that the growth, evangelism and church planting of the early church was facilitated and accelerated by the ministry gifts of the Holy Spirit and the development of helpful leadership structures. This chapter has sought to reflect on this and give principles that we would all do well to apply and reflect on *prior* to our planting rather than in retrospect.

If this is not done our church plants may need to start with being renewed rather than evangelising their areas.

Note

1. I am thankful to Martin Scott for his observations in this area.

PART 3

THE PRACTICALITIES OF CHURCH PLANTING

CHAPTER 9

NINE STEPS TO PLANTING A CHURCH

Having looked at some of the broad issues relating to the subject of church planting, we now want to identify various practical steps involved in the process. Obviously, there are many ways of planting church – far too many to cover within the boundaries of this volume! Alongside that, there are always the exceptions; situations which seem to be operating in ways that defy some of the key principles which we hold dear. God's wisdom is many-sided and his ways ingenious and diverse. We need to retain an openness to learn in these areas and have a flexible *modus operandi* which can be influenced, adjusted and developed. Pioneering will involve risk, experimentation and mistakes. The more we can learn from others in order to avoid these, so much the better.

In the light of this I would like to outline nine steps which are generally part of our process of church multiplication. The steps we suggest are as follows:

Receiving and imparting the vision, Developing methods and models, Identifying the area, Selecting and designing the team, Training the team, Preparing the ground,

Releasing resources, Forming a realistic strategy and goals and Facilitating ongoing development.

1. Receiving and Imparting the Vision

Effective church planting on an ongoing basis will be facilitated by a clear strategy. This strategy will flow from and be fuelled and occasionally interrupted by our vision from the Lord.

In our context, factors including scriptural study, prayer and prophetic words gave us a vision to church plant initially within our home county. Our strategising has involved the identification of around thirty of the most ripe communities in this immediate area and the plan to plant in those during the next ten years. Into this mix God has intervened, broadening our vision so that we are currently planting in a key city outside this area, which has in turn required further adjustments to our only recently formulated strategy.

This kind of development appears to have early church parallels. Their vision was the Great Commission (Mt 28:18–20). The broad strategy was Jerusalem, Judea, Samaria and the ends of the earth (Acts 1:8). Into this mix came divinely initiated changes to their more detailed strategic planning. The Macedonian call (Acts 16:6–10) is an example of this.

Once vision has been received and a strategy developed by leadership, it then needs to be communicated to and at times shaped by the wider church. This process needs to be carefully implemented. Leaders must not expect the rest of the church to apprehend in one evening, a vision which has been conceived during months of careful preparation.

Vision needs to be unpacked through preaching, teaching and exhortation at all our meetings. This needs to be at every level of church life, from main meetings through to members' gatherings, house groups and youth meetings. It also needs to be communicated relationally and expressed by all the gifts and ministries in the church: apostles building, prophets speaking into it, teachers teaching, evangelists growing it and pastors shaping and leading the community forward.

Corporate prayer, fasting and fund-raising also enable people to grasp and own all the church is doing – our aim being that each member should be actively involved, being able to articulate and own the vision in their own way and feeling they are able to contribute towards its fulfilment. As this is accomplished our growth will surely accelerate.

Envisioning our people transforms situations. Recently we were preparing two new congregational plants, one into a major city and another into a large village situation. The city seemed to be a door of opportunity while the smaller situation seemed to have more problems. We could not raise a full team for it and began to wonder whether we were moving too early. At this stage a member of our congregation, unaware of the situation, prophesied directly to us as leaders concerning the need to press on and not be afraid to move quickly – it was not the Lord who was slowing us down.

After weighing, we accepted the prophesy and with this in mind quickly communicated the vision to the church both at a members' meeting and then to the whole group on the Sunday. Suddenly the whole atmosphere changed, faith grew and we saw that the Lord was with us. We immediately had thirty people volunteer to move to the city and twenty-five into the village situation. We were in business and it was the careful impartation of the vision under God's hand that released the response which moved us forward.

As people own our broader vision many will feel called to be involved, at whatever level, in pioneering a new church. Some of them will have a burden for particular locations while others will be willing to go to wherever is most strategic.

One final key in this area is that we need to help those who are staying to feel part of the vision. They need to be able to identify with the process of nurturing the new group through prayer, regular updates and, for a few, direct involvement. It is also vital that as many as possible of those who don't go to plant do so because they feel a direct call to stay with the mother congregation. Those left need to maintain a vibrant sense of call and vision to continue the development of the sending group. If this is not the case our main resource congregations will be excessively weakened. This will in turn affect the resourcing of the new groups, and restrict the speed at which further church plants can be accomplished.

2. Developing methods and models

Chapters 5 and 7 have examined some of the biblical methods and models of church planting. In this more practical section I want to outline some of the means by which we have established new churches. There are other models of which I am aware, but here I want to describe ideas which we have thoroughly tested rather than sketch out models which we have only read about but never used.

Leadership

In all our church planting, the training, development and selection of appropriate leadership are of vital importance. Normally we would be training and grooming leaders of different types well in advance of any involvement they may have in leading a new congregation. They would be given opportunity and be shaped in the areas of their skills, relational capabilities, conceptual understanding and character.

With this in operation, ideally during the six months prior to the establishment of a new work, the embryonic core leadership can be drawn to one side and specifically prepared with the future project in mind. During this preparation we normally make it clear to this group and the rest of the church that they are an embryonic team, leading the plant on behalf of the whole church oversight team. This means they can relax, knowing they have our resources and support, and we also have time to observe the team on the ground, allowing them to be fully tested.

Sometimes prior to this process we will be clearly aware of who the breakthrough person (leader of leaders) will be and so we will provisionally reveal this. On other occasions it is more appropriate to let the new team pray, plan, lead meetings and perform all the duties of local leadership together without this definition. This short period with plenty of loose ends, enables them to thrash issues through and get to know one another a little better! While this is happening a member of the wider church oversight team is generally on hand to advise and be drawn in to help with any lock-up situations or relational difficulties.

Only when this process has run its course, and the new congregation has been established, will the leaders be confirmed and have hands laid on them in front of the whole church. This process normally takes between twelve and eighteen months.

Methodology

When church planting it is particularly important to establish a living cell of body life that is able to pioneer evangelistically and grow through conversions. This is far more readily achieved if a smaller group is planted into a new area rather than a large group being subdivided into area groups.

I know of several churches which have tried subdividing in this way only to regroup exclaiming that "congregations don't work". Within nature, if you want to plant a tree you will take a small cutting rather than saw the whole tree in half. A cutting will grow and prosper, leaving the 'donor' tree in an equally healthy state. Sawing in half will kill both the donor and the new 'branch'. Our planting needs to be strategic, planned and through groups of people who are going to build new work through evangelistic endeavour. Simply dividing your existing people up and meeting in different areas is not, to my mind, church planting until impact has been made in the new community and the discipleship of new converts begins to occur.

Small core beside locals

Often a situation emerges when people from another town begin to be converted and added to the church. In these cases we have at times encouraged them to become linked with an existing group in that area. However, sometimes this has proved difficult, and as these people have evangelised their friendship networks a number of others from this new area have been joined to the church.

In these cases we have trained a core group of leaders and they have then moved over into this new area to start a congregation alongside the locals.

When this type of plant is pursued we need to ensure that the group of locals has enough 'weight' to form a new work. If you decide that it is lacking, it may well then be worth rallying some other members of the mother congregation to move over in support. This action is infinitely preferable to establishing a new group that spends its early months and even years struggling to grow.

Whole group move

In other situations we have moved whole groups of people into a new area to plant. In an inner-city area it is easier to operate in a more gradual manner, and the cell multiplication method comes into its own.

However, when the new area is several miles away, credible church planting cannot be carried out without people moving house. In these situations an area within the new community is identified as the epicentre of the new church's planned activities. The people will then endeavour to locate their house move as strategically as possible within the area.

Cell multiplication

This is perhaps one of the fastest methods of reproducing congregations, particularly in an inner-city area of dense population. It is a method which has been particularly used by the Ichthus Fellowship in South London.

The idea is that each congregation has cell groups covering their area of operation. These groups are all operating evangelistically in this sphere. As time goes on a group of around three cells on the edge of the area (see figure 1) begins to evangelise in a new community. As converts begin to appear and they grow, these three cells can be taken to one side to form a new congregation. At this stage further leadership resources are usually sent to the new group to give them the weight needed to establish a new congregation.

The benefits of this model are obvious. It is much easier for the mother congregation to be planting more than one group at a time, and more quickly. People are not having to move house, and because you are hiving off existing cells the need for restructuring in the original group is minimalised. Alongside this, in a large congregation it is not inconceivable that two or even three groups of cells may be working towards a plant simultaneously. This model obviously reproduces more quickly than the whole group or core group methods.

Figure 1

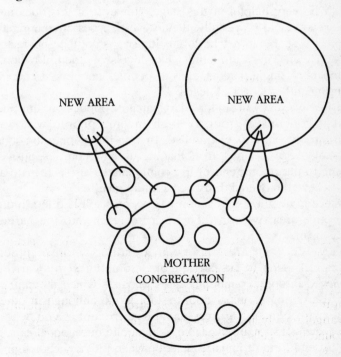

3. Identifying the Area

In order to maintain and develop an effective strategy for planting we need to analyse clearly the areas in which we plan to operate. Here I have set out some of the ways in which we do this.

(i)   First, it is helpful to know what the broad sphere of operation for our church-planting strategy is. This may be a group of towns, part of a county or a whole region.

(ii)   Within this area we then need to identify the key centres upon which we will focus. There are a number of ways in which this can be done. However, some initial ideas can be gained from obtaining copies of the local and regional census figures.

(iii)   We then need to define the criteria on which we will prioritise these areas. Obviously, a direct word from the Lord could be very helpful at this stage! However, if this does not occur we would prayerfully identify which types of community we feel best able to reach. Population size is not the only factor to consider. There are others like levels of unemployment, numbers of single parents, ages of people, amounts of council housing and other social needs.

Often we may encounter a large area of population, but find that it contains a group of high income people who are particularly hard to evangelise. In our initial planting it is generally wise to target areas that are usually more responsive. Going to the poorer end of the community is also a focus that we believe the overall thrust of Scripture gives us.

Once a vibrant congregation has been established in a more receptive area, we can then begin to reach into the harder areas nearby.

(iv)   When an area has been identified, more detailed research needs to be carried out. Sometimes this can be achieved through community questionnaires which the church can use during its initial door-to-door work, although in other cases the census figures may be sufficient. Even when adequate statistics are available, community questionnaires can be a useful form of initial contact between the new church and members of the local community.

In one of our recent church plants this type of research proved particularly effective. We identified that the local pub and video shop were places that most people frequented. Members of the congregation then obtained jobs in those places and house groups were closed early on pub quiz night in order that church members could attend and meet the locals. A Karaoke evening was arranged by the church for the pub which enabled further good relations to be built with the community. As a result of this and other activities, our name became known in the area.

This foundation of 'seed sowing' enabled the main thrust of our evangelism to be effective. The local census had revealed a large number of single-parent families. Our local questionnaires had borne this out and it was clear that a well-organised playscheme would serve the needs of the community and be an excellent vehicle for witness.

The whole church resourced this and we had around 100 kids for the week, 1,000 locals to a family fun day, and after the week we now have nearly ninety unchurched kids in our youth work. The contacts made continue to bear fruit and at Christmas the congregation of thirty-five had 130 non-Christians attend their pantomime! The door is now wide open for the congregation to reach these friendship networks which are now within their sphere of influence.

Researching these areas enables us to know where our people should be living in order to have a maximum impact in the area. It also helps us to know what kind of congregation we need to be looking to establish there, particularly in terms of cultural make-up, which in turn will influence the type of meetings we have, their time, location and content.

4. Selecting and designing the team

The make-up of the team and congregation will depend entirely on both the area we are intending to reach and also the type of congregation we are looking to establish.

Some new groups will be planted specifically to reach their immediate area and will as a by-product of their growth continue to give a significant proportion of their resources away to the wider vision. Our target is that each congregation will aim to release around 15-20% of its people resources annually into church planting. These are what we call 'in fill' congregations, planted with the evangelisation of a more compact area in mind.

Other new groups will be planted and built as potential resource/mother congregations. These would normally be allowed to grow larger before planting (160–200 as opposed to 70-120+), and we would hope to see a conglomeration of more strategic, broader ministries not just giving input, but being resident within them.

Their task is twofold. First, to carry out the thorough evangelisation of the immediate area, and secondly to be instrumental in the planting and resourcing of many other congregations within their region.

Volunteers

Once it is clear what kind of congregation is in mind, we will then look to build the team. Initially we would invite key people to join the leadership team and also others to join the plant as part of the congregation. Once their replies have been received we will then open the project to the whole church.

At this stage we would assert that volunteering does not guarantee inclusion into the team. Although a group of mixed age and Christian maturity is desirable, it is important that the embryonic congregation is not swamped by numbers of people who have extreme pastoral problems.

The new group needs to consist of people who can be released wholeheartedly into growth-related activities. With this in mind, we have at times asked people who need extensive amounts of pastoral time to remain in the mother congregation, even when they may live in the area to be covered by the new plant. Once they are on an even keel, and the new group is established, then these people can either join the congregation in their area or become part of another church plant if they so desire.

Within all of this we need to keep an eye on the gift/ministry mix within the new group. It is desirable to have a mixture of evangelistic, prophetic and teaching gifts, as well as adequate cover of small group leadership and worship.

5. Training the team

We have already covered the issue of training for a group of people about to embark on a church plant. Normally, we would draw them out of their house groups around three months prior to the launching of a new congregation, and in this context we would encourage them to begin praying and worshipping together. Specific modules of teaching are then given which are designed to equip the group for the special demands that it is about to experience.

These particular modules are designed to reinforce the overall ethos and direction of the church, applying the outward-looking pioneering instinct which is in place as a result of the discipleship thrust already present in the church. In most cases, when people respond to take part in a church-planting initiative, they are already, to a degree, motivated, so this course needs to aim at giving 'bed and banks' to the river of enthusiasm which is already flowing. The kinds of subjects generally covered include: The kingdom of God and church planting (see Chapter 2), The church and community (see Chapter 6), A pioneering vision (breaking new ground, developing faith), Spiritual warfare (see Chapter 4), Meaningful meetings in congregations and homes, The church and relationships and The functions of local church leadership.

Added to this would be specific training in evangelism in the areas of friendship, door to door, visitation and streetwork (both performance and cold contact), as well as in running community events.

On occasions, a church plant may find itself with some existing Christians who wish to join. They are already in the area, but are not members of the sending church. Once this has been cleared and worked through in relationship with their former churches, it is wise to give these people time to be drawn into the life and ethos of the sending church. It is obviously undesirable to see an embryonic grouping swamped out by transfer growth and in consequence prevented from accomplishing its primary evangelistic task.

In our situation, people transferring have sometimes resided in a nearby mother congregation which has helped them adjust to the change. Whether this is possible or not we would normally lead these people through a church membership or orientation course which we have called "The Church and You". This is designed to help people to understand our distinctives, ask questions of the leaders and decide whether or not they feel drawn to identify with us fully.

Subjects covered here include: What is the church?, Relationships in the church. Communion, baptism, the Bible, prayer and the Holy Spirit, Worship and giving, and The church, the kingdom and evangelism.

Once this course has been finished and people have talked it through personally with local leadership, they can then be drawn into the training module aimed particularly at the new, potential congregations.

6. Preparing the ground

It is important that as much preparation as possible, of both the team and the area concerned, is carried out before the work actually begins. Our preparation normally covers three areas.

(i) Contacting existing churches

We would normally spend a considerable amount of time, wherever possible, talking to all the church leaders in a new area. In a town or village this is often possible, although in a city the number of churches makes this unworkable. In these situations we look to spend time with the key leaders and hopefully gain access to a local Ministers' Fraternal to present our plans. We assure them that our desire is to reach the unevangelised and not to draw transfers from existing groups. We confirm our commitment to co-operation and relationship with existing groups and wherever possible to taking part in the local scene. This approach has minimalised the threat level and meant that most of our new plants have experienced excellent co-operation from any existing churches in their areas.

(ii) Spiritual warfare

Although I see three dimensions to this activity (prayer, proclamation and action), at this stage our focus would be on preparing the ground in prayer. Walks of prayer, half-nights of prayer and other activities are initiated by the new group, which endeavours to discern areas of need and enemy activity, as well as demonic obstacles which face the new plant. This is vitally important in securing a fruitful environment for the initial evangelistic activities.

(iii) Pre-evangelism/seed sowing

Before the new group commences activities or meetings in the new area, we often have an 'advanced party' of our evangelism team in operation. They would be doing door-to-door visitation, performance streetwork, surveys and cold contact evangelism. Alongside this they would often visit local shops and key places, seeking to engage the people of the community in friendly dialogue.

In one of our current church-planting situations this has been particularly effective. Local shopkeepers and people generally have been surprisingly receptive, and we have encountered a significant group of non-Christian teenagers who have requested that we set up a youth club for them. They have also asked us if we have anything they could do on a Sunday as this is a particularly boring day for them!

7. Releasing resources

As has already been mentioned, the development of a larger vision and the embarking on a church-planting strategy will require financial resourcing. Sacrificial giving will become a way of life for any church which decides to be a kingdom resource.

In the light of this, leaders will need to budget carefully in addition to teaching the church to give. Specific fund raising occasions may become necessary in order to release enough extra funding to facilitate hall rentals, release of new ministry, leadership training, social action projects, music equipment, as well as the regular commitments which affect the normal church budget.

Our teaching on giving needs to be imparted to the church in every area of its life. Generous giving needs to be seen as an integral part of normative discipleship and therefore needs to be taught at every level, from the foundation course through to leadership training. Due to lack of space here I am unable to outline in detail our teaching in this area. However, I would like to outline ten principles which would be foundational within it.

(*i*) Tithing is an Old Testament principle which is not reiterated in the New Testament. However, the principle of giving regularly to the work of God still applies (1 Cor 16:2).

(*ii*) Even in the Old Testament, when all the offerings were added together it is likely that they drew about 30% of an individual's income.

(*iii*) Tithing in the sense of 10% is therefore only a helpful minimum guideline, and as people begin to apply ongoing faith to their finances, giving may rise to a much higher percentage level of a person's overall income.

(*iv*) The emphasis in our giving should be on generosity (2 Cor 8:1–3) and in proportion to a person's total income (1 Cor 16:2). For a family on low pay, 10% may be a huge sacrifice when there is little disposable income. However, people on large incomes have more disposable resources and therefore are often more able to give a larger overall percentage.

(*v*) Giving must come cheerfully, from a free will decision and out of love for God and not for any other motive (2 Cor 9:7)

(*vi*) The firstfruits, or tithe, are laid 'at the apostles' feet' (Acts 4:35). This means that money is released without strings attached and is given to the church leadership to facilitate the vision of the whole church which these leaders are implementing. This tithe needs to be given as a priority to the church to which an individual belongs. This is the place where they receive their pastoral care and with whom they identify (as the whole of Israel supported the Levites).

(*vii*) If people would then like to release extra free will offerings to worthwhile causes, they can do so knowing they have fulfilled their primary responsibility.

(*viii*) Giving should be regular and planned (1 Cor 16:2), not haphazard. Presenting our 'firstfruits' to God is a priority, so giving to God should be the first thing we do when we receive our income.

(*ix*) As a result, where possible, standing orders are a worthwhile consideration because they do help leadership to budget effectively for future growth since they know how much is guaranteed to be given. Where standing orders are operated, individuals need to ensure that their giving does not just become another regular 'bill'. Faith and prayer need to be applied to it to ensure that it remains a part of our worship.

Covenanting all regular giving is also very helpful as all tax paid can be claimed back by churches who have charitable status (as such, every £1 given then becomes worth around £1.40).

(*x*) All church strategies and goals need to be costed and broken down before the whole church. In this way people can see the whole picture and own it prayerfully. This encourages both a personal response in faith, as well as corporate faith and prayer in the direction of extra resources.

8. Forming a realistic strategy and goals

In all of this activity I believe that it is essential for a new group to have clear measurable goals for growth in every area which relate to the first six to twelve months initially, and then further into the future. Having faith targets will give the group something specific to aim at before God and also, because they are measurable, it is possible as time goes on to evaluate where the congregation is at, whether it is moving forward or not, and if there are problems, to solve them as soon as possible.

Exceeding our goals is never a problem, and even falling short of them need not demotivate the group. We have very rarely reached our goals. We have, however, learned much along the way and moved forward considerably. Prayerfully considered goals should never be set in stone. However, they are a powerful motivation for us as we seek to move forward in God's purposes. It seems that the Apostle Paul himself had goals and that these propelled him into his many missionary and church-planting projects (Rom 15:20).

This setting of goals has had a positive effect on all our plants. The measurable nature of them has been a catalyst to us as we have continued to evaluate whether or not we have succeeded, and if not what kind of adjustments need to be made.

In our second church plant into central Bognor we aimed to grow from around eighteen people to seventy in the first year. We embarked on all kinds of aggressive evangelism and saw numbers of converts. However, we soon realised that the group there was too weak to disciple these people as many of the individuals already in the church had enough problems of their own! Some of these converts were lost and as we re-evaluated our goals we realised we were not going to achieve the numerical targets.

At this stage we encouraged and re-envisioned the leadership and congregation, and embarked on a process of training, developing and strengthening the group alongside the existing evangelism. This re-evaluation gave us the key to the situation and now the group is progressing well, numbering over 100 people and having sent several key individuals into other church-planting situations.

The third plant into North Chichester had an aim to reach fifty in the first year from their initial core of around twenty-five. Alongside this there were goals affecting prayer, prophecy and worship, as well as hitting the local community in depth and seeing converts through community social events and door-to-door work.

The numerical goals were fulfilled as were many of the others relating to prayer, prophecy and worship. Converts came from friendship contacts and the local teacher training college. However, the goals of biting deep into the local community still remain unfulfilled, although the group is still growing healthily and stands at around seventy people, having released a number (including leaders) into other church plants. Our efforts here are at present aimed at breaking through evangelistically, particularly along the lines of some of the original, as yet unfulfilled, goals.

The fourth plant into the Bersted area of Bognor which we described earlier, had specific evangelistic and community profile targets for the first year. The group which moved was very young and quite inexperienced, but had owned the vision with excitement, commitment and maturity. The small core quickly doubled to around thirty-five people and the sphere of friendships and hot contacts in the local area has far exceeded anything we could have imagined. However, the discipling and integration of these contacts into the local group has been slow and difficult. Therefore, goals have been adjusted and we are now refocusing on a clear reaping emphasis in our evangelistic work and putting more resources and time into discipling and integrating new people.

From these three examples I hope it can be seen that goals release energy and give people a focus for their faith. Also, when they are specific and measurable, the measuring process provides an invaluable opportunity to learn from any mistakes and focus on the perceived areas of need.

9. Facilitating ongoing development

A key to planting churches which in turn grow, mature and reproduce continually, is the whole area of ongoing development. Church planting is not over when a new group begins meeting and seeing new converts. Rather, it has only just begun.

New groups need to be resourced financially, as well as with preaching and teaching ministries from the resource congregations. And not only at a leadership level, but evangelistically too. This will ensure a healthy development, protection from the curse of parochialism and the maintenance of an ongoing vision and growth momentum.

In this context the planting of totally independent and autonomous groups is not something that I would regard as desirable, or biblical for that matter. It is clear that churches planted in New Testament times were established, nurtured, resourced and linked through an ongoing relationship with apostolic team ministry. Any move of church planting which fails to recognise this will be missing out on one of the most important aspects of biblical church planting (see Chapter 8).

However, moving towards this will be difficult for many in the short term. Therefore, when church planting, we need to ask ourselves, "Are we an embryonic movement or a church which finds its context within a stream or denomination?"

Groups which are becoming a movement still need to be 'networked' and find relationships, input and a measure of accountability outside their own contexts. These things provide a safeguard and many windows for us to learn from others. None of us has a monopoly on truth, and openness in these areas will be the hallmark of groupings which maintain their growth in the long term.

More independent churches need to be 'networked' in somewhere to give them a broader vision, accountability and access to a wider resource base. While more institutional or denominational models are not ideal from my perspective, some of them are infinitely preferable to the 'charismatic Brethrenism' which often leaves groups isolated, irrelevant and visionless.

Unfortunately, denominational models which rely on institutions, common practice, ordination and other religious rites to maintain their solidarity, often find it difficult to resource and develop their churches both relationally and spiritually. Apostolic ministry cannot be regionalised, organised or systemised. It relies on the anointing and gifting of the Holy Spirit and, like all other aspects of the New Testament church, it is charismatic (Holy Spirit given) and not institutional. Those operating in denominations are the best ones to face and solve these issues for themselves. I am glad of this because I do not see that there are any easy answers! However, that does not mean that we should not be asking the questions!

In any case, the ongoing resourcing and links with our established church plants are vitally important, both in terms of keeping them in a growth situation and also to allow them the privilege of releasing many of their people into the wider work of Great Commission church planting.

CHAPTER 10

TRAINING UP LEADERS

In the chapter on discipleship we observed some of the foundational elements of training and development within the Christian context. If applied on an ongoing basis to every aspect of our church life, these will begin to produce potential leaders. The task of the church is then to build on this and generate enough trained leadership to ensure a continued acceleration of its planting strategy. As we have already seen, the church can be the ideal context for producing leaders provided enough resources and care are invested in effective training modules.

In many cases the importance of training leaders can be overlooked. Moderate growth can be experienced and the occasional congregation planted without too much difficulty. It is only as growth increases that the lack of past investment in potential leadership comes home to roost, as the growth is obstructed by a leadership vacuum.

A recent survey within the Pioneer network of churches revealed how urgent this issue is. Most of the churches were growing effectively. The overall annual percentage growth of attenders was 17%. However, only one or two churches were producing leaders at the equivalent rate to their projected growth over the next ten years. The vast majority of others were facing a potential famine of leadership. It became clear to us that any growth strategy is likely to fail unless it incorporates aims, goals and a focus on leadership training.

The church – a training school

In the UK particularly, there needs to be a radical reassessment of our models of church if we are to produce enough leaders. The local church which relies exclusively on buying in leadership from a Bible college will never have enough leaders and will continually be like a family reeling from the loss of a parent. This grief cycle reoccurs continually as the professional type of leadership tends to take a promotional move to a bigger church every seven years or so. At this stage a new minister arrives, takes three years to settle in and just gets things up and running before moving on and plunging the church into the same cycle all over again!

Churches that have experienced a measure of success in this type of environment tend to have been 'teaching centres', those that have been built around the success of an individual personality. The problem with these often relatively large churches, is that they tend to produce 'pew fodder' – well-taught, mature Christians often frustrated by the lack of opportunity to be developed in a context where the gap between the small number of key leaders and any potential trainees is widening continually. In this environment the opportunities to reproduce ministry, especially those involving preaching, are restricted.

Providing opportunities

The training of leaders will mean that 'corks' need to be taken out of the bottles. Key ministry will need to be prepared to give time to the training of others and vacate their pulpits for long periods. This will cause some to experience an identity crisis as they learn to focus on facilitating others rather than doing it all themselves. Also, more established members of the flock will have to be patient as trainees experiment on them! Hopefully they themselves will be too busy stepping out in faith in other areas to consider taking the position of the armchair critic!

Locally we spent much time as we began church planting, thinking of the best structure to facilitate training. The 'mega-church' model alone did not seem to fit our requirements. It was only as we observed the work of Ichthus that we encountered the cell, congregation and celebration model. I am not saying that this is the model for all occasions, but I would like to explain how it has worked for us and then discuss leadership training in that context. The reason for this is that if we fail to incorporate a flexible model which creates room for trainees first, our leadership training may only be preparing people for frustration.

Celebration

This is a meeting on a regular basis (weekly in Ichthus, monthly in the Revelation context), designed to draw all the congregations together for an envisioning, teaching and 'mega' focus of church. Large gatherings of believers provide a sense of focus and belonging to something larger and significant which can make waves of impact into the local area. These gatherings are generally more impersonal (due to their size), but provide a focus for the best and most experienced available ministry. As such it gives very little room for emerging leadership.

Congregations

These are smaller, more household and family-orientated groupings which operate into a defined local sphere, proclaiming the gospel of the kingdom into that context. Being anything from around 60 to 180 people there is a more intimate feel about them and they provide a more appropriate context for emerging ministry. As new groups of this type are planted, gaps emerge within both the mother congregation and the new group. The dynamic of the smaller setting is less threatening and an ideal environment for the first few steps into public leadership!

Cell

These are groups of between twelve and twenty people who meet within the local area of their congregation. They express the wider vision of the church in 'micro' form and are the cornerstones of both our evangelistic and pastoral strategy. They also provide an ideal forum to train all types of ministry and leadership in its earlier stages.

Having established a flexible model which we felt created enough opportunities for training, we then needed to develop a complementary leadership structure which gave opportunity, while maximising all our key resources. As such we began to develop three spheres of leadership within our church: oversight, congregational leadership and cell leadership.

Oversight

This was the group that provided the key visionary and directive thrust for the whole church. This group would, in liaison with the congregational leaders, develop the overall strategy which could then be outworked and contextualised by each congregation. The focus of the whole church would be the celebration meetings, out from which the congregations would flow. This prevents a parochial mindset from developing within the local congregations which in the long term will inhibit growth.

This leadership group performs an apostolic function to the congregations, providing them with key ministry resources on an ongoing basis. In this way none of our congregational plants has so far become autonomous, which means that financial resources are held centrally. As a result, when we plant into new areas the emerging church is financially resourced and draws personnel from the wider church, which means all congregations have the opportunity to contribute to our church planting. In this way the whole process accelerates because we are all united in our involvement, and the key ministry resources that have been given to previous plants can be drawn upon to enhance other congregations. This creates further space within their home congregation for others to develop.

With this in mind most of our leadership training would also operate centrally, as would our evangelism, social action and other teams. This means we can offer a far higher standard and deploy our key resources more strategically.

Congregational leadership

These leaders are responsible for the 'earthing' at grass roots level of the wider vision. They will carry responsibility for the pastoral work, most of the preaching and indeed all the day to day running of the congregation. They will be training and developing emerging leadership of all types and plugging into all the wider church training initiatives as a supporting resource.

Cell leadership

These will operate as previously defined with each cell normally having one or two 'helpers' who are being groomed for future leadership.

Training modules

With an overall model which aims to create maximum opportunity and release key ministries to train, we are then able to develop appropriate training modules. In our experience these have to be continually adjusted in line with our changing requirements and also lessons learnt.

At present we operate a basic Leadership Training course which every person who has any kind of responsibility in the church needs to complete. Initially it was run over a period of two months but we found that this shorter period of time gave less opportunity for the material to 'sink in' and be earthed practically in experience.

Therefore we would now run the fifteen sessions over a six month period and have organised a tutorial system whereby all material is subsequently worked through on a 'one to one' basis with subject related tasks also being set. With this system in place we have found that more of the content slips from 'head to heart' and that fewer issues need to be re-emphasised at a later date.

Around this basic training other specialist courses have developed to impart skills relating into various aspects of church life. The evangelism team, Youth team, childrens team, Social Action team, Pastors, Preachers and administrators have all been given locally based training. On top of this our whole leadership team (all who hold any responsibility) will meet regularly on a congregational basis for teaching, dialogue and the maintenance of vision. The ongoing discipleship, in concert with these modules means people are developing continually in their theological and conceptual understanding whilst being given the necessary practical skills to function in leadership.

Into this mix we have found it necessary to expose our key leadership at some stage to a more concentrated and lecture-based form of theological training. As such we have developed 'Equipped to Lead' which is run by the Pioneer Team on a national basis. With prepared course notes and a larger budget, we have been able to use the best of our own speakers and import key specialists to provide input to a course which covers an extensive range of theological/leadership related issues in depth.

Continued and accelerated church planting will also create a demand for more full-time personnel, or others who can release longer periods of time to be trained and be involved in pioneering new churches. This kind of training can concentrate on producing evangelists and 'break-through' leaders to resource the new plants. Examples of this kind of training are the Ichthus Network summer projects and also their year-long teams. Pioneer also operates short-term and long-term TIE teams which have to date trained and released a number of significant evangelists/church planters into the network of churches.

Mentoring and shaping

We have already observed that in the ministry of both Jesus and Paul there were individuals who were trained at a more personal and intimate level. There are certain things that can only be received when given in a relational, more one-to-one environment where people feel free to ask questions and talk things through in depth. There may also be certain 'home truths' from the mentor's perspective that are more appropriately shared in the context of this kind of relationship!

As a result, to a greater or lesser degree most people in our church are being 'mentored' by a more mature Christian in some way or other. Certainly as an individual begins to show signs of real potential we would strategically link them with a key ministry in the church who can then begin to invest quality time in them. In this we would not want to create a one-to-one exclusive discipling relationship. We recognise that over a period of time we are all likely to reproduce not just our strengths, but also our weaknesses! So, a mentoring situation may last for an extended period, and while the relationship and contact continue, the trainee may be linked into another person who will look to shape different aspects of their life.

An example of this would be how I have often worked with Pete Gilbert who is a key evangelist and trainer. He has an incredible ability to take a person with raw potential and equip them to function in ministry, honing their gifts amazingly quickly, as well as getting to the heart of them in terms of the key issues of discipleship. He can do this in a way that I cannot.

However, too long with him and the person is likely to miss out on some of the broader aspects of leadership and become a little one-dimensional. Therefore, with this in mind, they would then be released to spend time with me. I could never give anyone initial training to the degree that Pete is able to, but I can begin to pick up on broader issues of leadership, character and development which flow naturally from my strengths. This kind of 'team mentoring' is far more effective than claustrophobically locking people up with an individual, which is an arrangement with many pitfalls.

Within the process of mentoring it is important to find forums in which people can work together, whether this is just 'carrying the bags' of a more senior person on an extra-local sortie, or working with them on an ongoing project. Locally we have sought to ensure that wherever possible every exercise of church leadership includes the drawing in of a learner who can observe and at times share in the work.

My wife Margaret is an absolute master in this area of training, having developed an extremely effective way of shaping pastoral leadership in the context of our new Christians group. This is a model that we have also reproduced in other areas of our church.

In the context of the group there is one 'trainee' pastor for every two or three new converts. Margaret would meet with these trainees on a bi-weekly basis to set them tasks in the care of their people. They will meet them for a meal at least once a week and spend time getting to know them, working through the basic material on the course. Each trainee will provide regular detailed feedback on how things are going and at that stage Margaret will give perspectives on how well (or badly) the situation is being handled. Issues that need facing are identified and advice is given on how they should be tackled. Should a situation of real complexity emerge then Margaret would handle it, usually alongside the trainee.

In this way she is able to help the trainee develop a wide range of relational, pastoral and other skills, as well as giving over small parts of the teaching within the group, when appropriate. Many of these helpers are now in key areas of leadership within the church. Their growth has been maintained because of the foundations laid in these early stages of their development.

Key leadership

Once people begin to enter into a measure of responsibility and become competent in leadership and ministry, it is important that we do not then neglect them, concentrating on emerging ministry exclusively. If we do this we will be creating potential bottlenecks in the church. Folk who are functioning extensively need to feel valued, resourced and that they have an environment to unload into and be cared for. This can particularly apply in larger congregations.

To cover this and supplement the ongoing relationships that exist, we split our leadership team into groups of three to five, allocating a group to each congregational leader. In the context of each leadership team meeting we will have an extended time when these groups assemble to share more deeply in relationship, prayer, feedback and input. Personal issues arising can then be picked up by the congregational leader at a later time if appropriate. In this environment leadership team members hopefully feel valued and resourced, and know that they have clear access to a congregational leader at all times if needed.

In this vein, a gap can often emerge between the function of key leadership team members and the congregational leadership/eldership forum. People have learned all they can without actually being exposed to the 'eldership experience'. Church plants are being planned and strategised, yet there is a lack of people who've actually had hands-on experience of local church leadership.

When faced with this problem, the best solution is not always to appoint new elders, or even identify trainees. To do this too early can often be a mistake. On certain occasions we have solved this by drawing 'trainee trainees' into our congregational leadership forums! It is suggested to an individual that at some stage there may be a possibility of them training for congregational leadership or some other function. To test the waters in this area, we would invite them to attend the congregational leaders' meetings, take part in the debates, carry out certain tasks and enjoy the hot seat of prayer and personal input which often occurs at these forums!

With no strings attached the person can be observed and helped, and they can honestly express their feelings. In our context the vast majority will go on to be trained and become congregational leaders in our church plants, while others may share in another area of leadership.

Five processes of development

As I have embarked on numerous mentoring relationships in the church context, I have often found it helpful to focus on five processes of development which I have sought to see in operation as I interacted with an individual. These together, I feel, will bring a balance and stability into their personal growth.

1. Impartation

As we begin to relate, I believe that it is essential to bear in mind that our teaching should be formation, not information. In the words of Roger Forster, "Most things are caught not taught!" In our time together we need to share who we are with people. This opening up gives people a window to see into our lives and learn accordingly.

Bob Mumford talks about the law of mumps and measles. You may tell an individual that you have mumps. You may teach him about mumps. But in the end, if you have measles that is what he will catch! We must not expect to be able to teach people about relationships and accountability, for instance, if we are not ourselves living in those things already. The role of example will be key in these areas.

Also, we need to concentrate on imparting our heart and ethos as kingdom people. For example, if issues of pride or legalism are encountered, time needs to be taken to impart the Spirit of Christ and see a change of heart. Often this change may be invisible outwardly. However, it may become obvious, for instance, that for the first time a person is being motivated towards spiritual discipline out of God's love and grace rather than out of guilt and a need to earn acceptance.

The area of impartation is also vital in the development of ministry gifts. Rubbing shoulders with a more mature ministry is sure to release growth, and also the laying-on of hands at appropriate moments may well impart new areas of gift (2 Tim 1:6).

2. Building

Mentors are architects. They see the overall plan and are prepared to commission a wide range of skilled people to finish the job. There is a building process that needs to take place, not only in the church, but also in the lives of individuals (Eph 4:16). Therefore, we need to have a strategy in mind for each person – starting with the foundations of their life and working upwards.

An example of this would be a couple who came to us following a short time with a Christian mission organisation. They expressed a long-term desire to be sent out into overseas church planting. I sat with them and we discussed what building bricks would need to be in place for this to occur. Together, we decided that local church leadership training followed by small group leadership and evangelism team experience was step one. Step two was congregational leadership and then involvement in the pioneering of a new church plant.

During this process the couple will be asking the Lord which nation they need to focus on and when this becomes clearer we could together pursue any open doors, maybe a short- to medium-term visit, and specific cross-cultural training to pave the way for a longer-term involvement.

A building plan gives people a sense of progress and a long-term focus. This can be an impetus in working through some of the nitty-gritty issues of character which will need to be breached in order to keep moving forward.

3. Shaping
This involves exhortation, encouragement, rebuke and comfort, which from a Pauline perspective, appears to be the stuff of church life. We need to be constantly looking at people's gifts and talents, seeing how best they can be honed and shaped. Constant feedback, positive criticism, questions and ongoing advice need to be regular features of our time together.

Also, in this context we need to have a secure enough relationship for there to be the opportunity to hone unhelpful character edges, thus helping folk to progress in wholeness.

4. Broadening
Emerging leadership needs continually to be encouraged to see the many-sided wisdom of God. Just watching a new

157

leader coming to terms with some of the paradoxes in Scripture, for instance, is an exciting, rewarding and often amusing experience! In moving on into responsibility keen young Christians sometimes lose their 'spiritual virginity'. Their naïveté is often demolished as they encounter some of the pastoral difficulties, disappointments, pressures and criticisms of leadership. In these moments we need to be on hand to strengthen, support and comfort. These often painful times can be the richest opportunities for people to broaden in their understanding.

A recent situation comes to mind when one of our most promising younger church plant leaders was involved in some extra-local ministry as part of a team. The receiving church asked for honest feedback as to how best they could move forward in evangelism and what were the obstacles they needed to overcome. My protégé proceeded to write a five-sided penetrating analysis of the church situation which was both perceptive and probably at least 90% accurate. It would, however, have destroyed the leaders concerned! Fortunately, in openness he showed me the letter at draft stage and I was able to adjust it, reduce it by at least 50% and make it considerably more subtle and gentle. He learned a lesson in letter-writing and the receiving church obviously appreciated it, sending him a reply which commented on his maturity and sensitivity!

5. Maintaining

In a nurture and growth situation, often the new experiences, accelerating learning curve and other pressures can create an energy gap. Our involvement in mentoring is aimed at developing leadership who can run the race from start to finish and who will be there taking responsibility and standing firm when others have shrunk back from the task.

To achieve this we will need to be continually monitoring how people are doing, identifying problems, recognising that for many there may be periods when hyperactive functioning is inappropriate and that time needs to be taken to build somewhat more foundationally in their lives and relationships.

In all of this a focus on development in character is essential. This needs to be happening in at least three areas.

First, the area of wholeness and healing. We need to be helping our trainees to come to terms with their past, present and future. Hurts from their upbringing, past relational wounds, security and identity problems and other of life's scars will inhibit leadership maturity. The skilful mentor will be able to bring others to the place of receiving God's healing in order that they can lead from a position of wholeness and not end up subject to the oft-repeated scenario of the leader projecting his own weaknesses onto the people.

Secondly, there will need to be a development in the area of servanthood, humility and teachability. Unhelpful attitudes need to be challenged and people brought to the place where they are truly responding to the calling of God to serve rather than being driven by any need for acceptance or status.

Thirdly, we need to help people in areas of their self-control, self-expression and self-discipline. This will lead us to talking through areas of appetite, sexuality, relational and communication abilities, as well as the devotional life.

The focus of our training and mentoring should be to produce whole people of character, who are committed to the investment of their whole lives into seeking first God's kingdom and serving the wider body of Christ. I hope that this chapter will have given some introductory pointers to help us in that.

CHAPTER 11

PRACTICAL THEOLOGY

Developing a theology and maintaining the quality of understanding and interaction in the church.

The ordinary person assumption

While recognising the extraordinary skills of the apostles and gospel writers, including particularly their historical, theological and literary expertise, it is vital to remember that both they and their Lord were mainly without special training or educational background. The Jewish leaders were nonplussed "as they observed the confidence of Peter and John, and understood that they were uneducated and untrained men" (Acts 4:13).

When teaching in his home town, Jesus' own contemporaries and relatives

> "became astonished, and said, 'Where did this man get this wisdom, and these miraculous powers? Is not this the carpenter's son? Is not His mother called Mary, and His brothers, James and Joseph and Simon and Judas? And His sisters, are they not all with us? Where then did this man get all these things?'" (Mt 13:54–56).

Even Paul, undoubtedly a professionally trained Pharisee, stated unequivocally:

> Where is the wise man? Where is the scribe? Where is the debater of this age? Has not God made foolish the wisdom of the world? For since in the wisdom of God the world through its wisdom did not come to know God, God was well-pleased through the foolishness of the message preached to save those who believe (1 Cor 1:20–21).

Given these New Testament descriptions it follows that no higher educational qualifications, let alone any academic theological training, are necessary to mature spiritual leadership in the church or in any church-planting programme. In fact these lines of training can be a considerable hindrance. They tend to remove people from the experiences of everyday lives of ordinary people and carry with them the status, power and money overtones that separate the rich and powerful from the poor and deprived in society, who are the proper priority for the gospel.

This is by no means to exclude those who are called and equipped for higher education from embarking on it. We need Christians in higher education to carry the gospel to the students and academics who are in spiritual poverty. The academic study of theology is a valid form of apologetics, of understanding and communicating the gospel to other academics who need it. Furthermore, an academic education is often the doorway into positions of authority and leadership in government and commerce, where we need Christians to be as salt and light in a dark world.

Where people have special intellectual ability and the opportunity to expand it, we must encourage them to develop their expertise as gifts to the body for the work of the kingdom. Nevertheless, the church must always be the place where the world order is overturned and where a truly biblical theology and training for ministry are open to all. Too often the opposite has happened and the world order has penetrated the church, thereby halting its mission and undermining its message. Paul reminds the Corinthians:

> Consider your calling, brethren, that there were not many wise according to the flesh, not many mighty, not many noble; but God has chosen the foolish things of the world to shame the wise, and God has chosen the weak things of the world to shame the things which are strong, and the base things of the world and the despised, God has chosen, the things that are not, that He might nullify the things that are, that no man should boast before God (1 Cor 1:26–29).

If those whom God is calling to spiritual leadership in his church and kingdom are mainly not among the wise and powerful in the educational and social terms of this world, we have to make sure we are giving them the right input and training which will qualify them to fulfil the highest possible calling for a man or woman – namely leadership in the work of God.

During my own past academic training, one of the worst pieces of absurdity I can ever remember being presented with was the claim that ordinary working men and women cannot understand what is termed 'conceptual language'. This is a great insult to ordinary people, and fortunately one which Jesus obviously rejected. Concepts such as fulfilment, satisfaction, sin, kingdom, salvation, eternal life and the symbols and parables of everyday life to which concepts readily lend themselves were the substance of his teaching. It was the academic Nicodemus who fought with the clarity of the concept of "new birth", whereas the socially outcast woman at the well had no real trouble with "living water"!

At the heart of the gospel is the concept of incarnation; of the word become flesh. As John puts it, "And the Word became flesh, and dwelt among us, and we beheld His glory, glory as of the only begotten from the Father, full of grace and truth" (Jn 1:14). If we can help ordinary men and women to grasp this most fundamental theological truth – simple yet profound – and to handle the Scriptures rightly in the light of it, expressing the same incarnational attitude to truth and action that God himself has done for us in Christ, then we will have exploded the heart of the gospel among them in just the way God intended. This is our task!

Jesus-centred theology

True theology always begins with evangelism: "Go therefore and make disciples of all the nations... teaching them ..." (Mt 28:19–20). At the heart of evangelism is Jesus Christ. So all genuinely Christian theology must have Jesus Christ at the centre. Evangelism brings the good news that sins are forgiven and the kingdom of heaven is received through faith in Jesus Christ. It is through faith in him that all else comes. A person is not saved through their own good works, nor through faith in a religious tradition, nor even through faith in the Bible as a religious book. A person is saved when they put their trust in the living Christ. At the beginning they may not know much about him, or about what is happening to them. But he is full of love and mercy and longs for a relationship with them. So he is not so much concerned about right mental belief to begin with, but about the state of the heart.

So, although theology does deal with reasonable, understandable statements about God and his ways, it too must begin with faith in Jesus if it is to be valid or worthwhile at all. It was this that Jesus had to emphasise to the Jewish leaders of his day: "You search the Scriptures, because you think that in them you have eternal life; and it is these that bear witness of Me; and you are unwilling to come to Me, that you may have life" (Jn 5:39–40).

Paul made this very clear to Timothy when he spoke of the Scriptures "which are able to give you the wisdom that leads to salvation through faith which is in Christ Jesus" (2 Tim 3:15). A person is saved through faith in Christ Jesus and no theology will bring revelation and understanding unless it is through faith in Christ Jesus as well. We evangelicals emphasise that this isn't faith in just "any Jesus", but the living Jesus of the Gospels, who died and rose again. Or, to put it at its simplest, whether a person has consciously understood it yet or not, he is saved when he puts his faith in the Jesus Christ of the New Testament Gospels as being both the Jesus of history and the God of eternity. He then discovers him to be real, his sins to be forgiven and the kingdom of heaven to be his inheritance.

Such a person starts out his Christian life with a potentially very clear theology. He has excellent grounds to take the good news accounts of Matthew, Mark, Luke and John seriously as God's truth. He then discovers that the Jesus he has met on their testimony also gives his authority to the Old Testament writings, which until that point he may have had considerable problems with accepting. Jesus said, "Do not think that I came to abolish the Law or the Prophets; I did not come to abolish but to fulfill. For truly I say to you, until heaven and earth pass away, not the smallest letter or stroke shall pass away from the Law, until all is accomplished" (Mt 5:17–18). It is also discovered that Jesus gives his authority to the rest of the New Testament Scriptures: "The Helper, the Holy Spirit, whom the Father will send in My name, He will teach you all things, and bring to your remembrance all that I said to you" (Jn 14:26). The person has discovered experimentally that the Christ of the gospels is alive. He has found him to be the Word of God incarnate. Everything He said and did – his way, his kingdom – is both the revelation of the character and image of God and the intended pattern for human beings to live by through faith in him.

As a person develops a dynamic relationship with God he comes to trust him more and the Gospels more. As he desires to grow in his relationship with him, and to obey him in every area of life he discovers that the Old Testament which prepared for and foreshadowed Christ is a resource which massively expands the Gospels. Similarly, the rest of the New Testament through which the Gospel witnesses and their colleagues recorded and applied the growth and development of the life and kingdom of Jesus becomes a further resource for knowing and obeying him.

Looked at this way, the primary basis of theology is the incarnation of Jesus. The primary source is the Gospels. So the dynamic interplay between the obedient believer in the church in today's world, the person of Christ encountered today in the Holy Spirit, and the written Gospel accounts becomes the essential quality of daily life for a Christian. This triangle is the fundamental basis of theology. The Old Testament and the rest of the New Testament are the proper preparation and expansion of the Gospel records and carry the full authority of Jesus. So the task of the church-planting team is to live true to this dynamic and to train new believers to understand and develop a simple theology through the grid of this basic triangle.

The believer in the church in today's world

The revelation of Jesus Christ, both in the Scriptures and in the Holy Spirit today, is directed at individual people who are part of God's corporate people, his body, and who have a particular missionary task to the current generation of today's society. So while agreeing without question that the Scriptures are the authoritative word of God, we can't understand them or obey them properly without doing so in the context of our place in the church in today's world.

Three things follow from this. First we must make sure that people are able to read and engage with the Scriptures for themselves. Tragically few people are able to do this easily at first without help. Those who have a Western higher education often carry either an open or hidden humanism and scepticism about the biblical worldview. Furthermore, many ordinary people from both the Western and so-called Third Worlds are less than fully literate and lack confidence in their ability to understand and formulate judgements for themselves. It is up to the church-planting team to tackle these obstacles, both by encouraging Bible reading and by working to restore a true sense of value and confidence in those who have been robbed of it. We have found it to be essential to get alongside people on a one-to-one basis to achieve this, as well as to tackle the obstacles in prayer and spiritual warfare.

Secondly, we must make sure that people understand the vital part that the church has in the plan of God, and that while truth is vital, it is undermined if it is applied without love, or in a way which is detrimental to the kingdom of God. Jesus apparently agreed with what the Pharisees of his day said, for example "All that they tell you, do and observe, but do not do according to their deeds" (Mt. 23:3), but described them as "liars" (Jn. 8:44) and blind guides who led people into a pit (Mt. 15:14). Paul emphasised, "Knowledge makes arrogant, but love edifies" (1 Cor. 8:1) and "If I … know all mysteries and all knowledge … but do not have love, I am nothing" (1 Cor. 13:2).

I will never forget the public censure and harsh treatment of a youth leader in a church I once attended, for asserting an extinction position on the fate of the lost. To this day I remember observing how like Jesus he was in the way he took his public censure, and how it helped me to take his position seriously, and how unlike Jesus the church leaders were, which made it hard for me to agree with anything they said. Those of us who are in positions of leadership and authority in church-planting situations need to make sure that the way we teach and lead facilitates and releases people to grow in theological understanding rather than over-value our wisdom and gifting and become too dependent on us as a source of knowledge. Sometimes this requires self-conscious humility and the very opposite of the self-promotion and emphasis on educational qualifications, books we've read or places we've been, that often marks the world's way of doing things.

Thirdly, we need to help people to take the world seriously, making the distinctions John makes between loving the world system and its ways (which we are not to do): "Do not love the world, nor the things in the world" (John 2:15), and loving and serving the world and its people (which is what we are all about): "For God so loved the world, that He gave …" (Jn. 3:16). God made the world, and the whole creation is waiting for Christians to take it seriously and grow up: "For the creation waits with anxious longing for the revealing of the sons of God" (Rom. 8:19). God loves men and women of all races, cultures and classes. "He made from one, every nation of mankind to live on all the face of the earth" (Acts 17:26). God must not be separated from his creation or his creatures. The incarnation makes everything potentially holy, for in Christ God became part of the creation and a member of the human race. So there can be no sacred and secular, rather there is a theological perspective on everything.

We must beware of holding this in theory, but not in practice. The earlier chapter on the kingdom makes this clear in many practical ways. Suffice it to say that the church planter needs to avoid the pitfall of assuming that the only important thing is planting churches as if this were an end in itself. Church exists, as we have already noted, to unlock the kingdom of heaven in the earth. So the church planter or leader must train him or herself to take a vital interest in all aspects of the creation, and in all aspects and activities of human life. Of course, no one could or should know about everything or be involved in everything. But the development of good team leadership encourages and must make room for a full-orbed variety of people and gifts suited to the multi-faceted richness of the human race and its environment.

We have found it very helpful to set up small working groups from time to time to shine the Scripture onto aspects of life which we find to have been neglected. At different times we have set up working groups on dance, the Third World, physical healing, money, business, alternative lifestyle, education, social work, to name only some. These then report back to the leadership team, with recommendations to spread knowledge and expertise throughout the whole body and to take whatever appropriate action follows.

The person of Christ encountered in the Holy Spirit today

For the reason that the Jesus of Scripture is alive today, theology is not just formulating or evaluating rational statements about the incarnate God. Nor is it limited to the study of biblical texts. Rather it is about knowing God and submitting our understanding and study to his person and his work as the truth unfolds. It is about discovering whether our understanding so far is right or not, and adapting and changing where it is not in order to progress on to further revelation. The tendency of reflection and study is always to look backwards. It is our task to make sure that it is directed at the present in order to achieve the purposes of God.

This is the purpose of the risen Christ, as he expressed it to his disciples at the eve of the planting of the Jerusalem church: "It is not for you to know times or epochs which the Father has fixed by His own authority; but you shall receive power when the Holy Spirit has come upon you; and you shall be My witnesses both in Jerusalem, and in all Judea and Samaria, and even to the remotest part of the earth" (Acts 1:7–8).

We must make sure that study and reflection never become an ivory-towered business, but are led only by those who have either a missionary heart or missionary gift and who are themselves in living daily contact with Jesus and involved in the job of the kingdom of God.

While admitting that in our experience we have at times needed to make sure that room was given to adequate thought, reflection and study in the course of the work of the kingdom, this imbalance only occurred in reaction to the paralysing effects of so much theological training and academic study which past generations of Christianity have suffered from. We must prevent this paralysis from overtaking contemporary church planting. As well as making sure that those who give a theological lead are gospel hearted and gospel practitioners, we need to make sure that all study is undertaken in the context of ongoing evangelism in the broad sense of the words, works and wonders that we have already considered. A great deal of learning can, and needs to, take place in the local context of church planting work rather than away from it.

Our own training programmes – where part of the day or week is spent in study and part in practical work – have to some extent pioneered the way in the contemporary church scene. Even where full-time residential courses away from the local church-planting context are necessary because of the need to cover large amounts of study quickly, or because of the staying power of already established institutions, it is vital to provide frequent periods of practical work placement in order to apply and test the on-the-ground viability of the teaching in day-to-day obedience to Jesus.

It also follows that practical theological study needs to be carried out in the context of the personal disciplines of worship, prayer and fasting through which the living Christ is encountered in the Holy Spirit. Both our study times and the practical outworking need to be interspersed with planned periods for these disciplines or else they will be squeezed out under the time pressure of study timetables and work goals. But they are the lifeline to revelation and success, and the only antidote to the kind of paralysis that study and activity for their own sake can all too easily cause.

The Gospel records and the rest of Scripture

In defining the nature of church in Chapter 1, we saw how the revelation of Jesus is fundamental to it. "And Simon Peter answered and said 'Thou art the Christ, the Son of the living God.' And Jesus answered and said to him, 'Blessed are you, Simon Barjonah, because flesh and blood did not reveal this to you, but My Father who is in heaven. And I also say to you ... upon this rock I will build My church'" (Mt 16:16–18). Given that this is the basis of church, it is hardly surprising if the way church planters approach the Scriptures is on the same basis – by the revelation of Jesus.

The word used by many theologians for a method of interpreting Scripture is "hermeneutic". The simple theology that we are recommending for church planting is the "gospel of Jesus" method, or "hermeneutic". This is to say that the revelation of Christ as recorded in the Gospel accounts becomes the tool for all biblical interpretation.

This can also be described as a "Gospel primacy" method, because it asserts that the Gospels come first in our understanding of the rest of Scripture. As we have already clearly emphasised, all Scripture is given authority by Jesus, so this is not to say that other parts are less reliable or authoritative than the Gospels. Rather, the point made in this method is that one part of Scripture, namely the Gospel records, needs to be used to interpret the rest properly. Given that this is the part which reveals the fullness of the incarnation, the word made flesh, it is by definition the written word about the word made flesh. So it makes obvious sense to interpret the rest by means of it.

If we take the example of a microscope or telescope where a special lens needs to be inserted in order to see the subject under view correctly, then the Gospel revelation of Jesus becomes our lens for properly seeing the rest of Scripture. In this way we are preserved from becoming sub-Christian neo-Jews or legalistic Christians who attempt to apply the New Testament pattern of church life like the propositions of a theoretical textbook. Instead, we are thrown back onto the person of Christ and the revelation of the Holy Spirit.

This is a very simple process to apply and one which very ordinary Christians can do, and yet it has profound scope. Jesus is learned and understood more and more in the Gospels to be applied to the whole of the rest of Scripture with its astonishing coverage of mankind and God in relationship in his creation in so many different societies and contexts.

Jesus himself used this method of interpreting the Old Testament. In the Sermon on the Mount he explained how he fulfilled the law in every detail: "Do not think that I came to abolish the Law or the Prophets; I did not come to abolish, but to fulfill. For truly I say to you, until heaven and earth pass away, not the smallest letter or stroke shall pass away from the Law, until all is accomplished" (Mt. 5:17–18). He then proceeded to explain how this smallest letter and stroke were upheld: "You have heard that it was said, 'An eye for an eye and a tooth for a tooth.' But I say to you, do not resist him who is evil; but whoever slaps you on your right cheek, turn to him the other also" (Mt. 5:38–39).

Now we may ask how this second statement is the literal fulfilment of the former, but Jesus says it is! So we place Jesus' statement and the rest of his life demonstrated in the Gospels over the Old Testament teaching. Then we see that it is less in outworking than Jesus' totally unconditional forgiving, but the same in root. Putting Jesus' life next to it as the fulfilment, puts the statement in the right direction for interpretation. We ask the question, "In what way is an eye for an eye and a tooth for a tooth radically loving?" The answer has to be that it is a lot more loving than taking out all the eyes and all the teeth of everyone in the family, tribe, or nation of the person who put out the original eye or tooth. It states that the punishment must fit the crime and not be disproportionate to it or over-harsh. It limits either judgement or vengeance in the direction of love and mercy. Jesus came to take the full effects of all vengeance and judgement so that no human being who trusts him needs to take action himself.

The historian A J P Taylor reckons that the First World War started mainly as a result of a young teenager putting out the eye of the Archduke of Sarajevo. If that was the case, a bit of Old Testament loving law would have saved a great deal of international carnage. Jesus' love goes further still!

This kind of biblical exegesis gives great practical help in many typical contemporary church-planting situations. I well remember a controversy in a church-planting team over how to deal with a pastoral issue relating to a new convert. A divorced lady who had lived with a difficult common law husband for many years since her divorce, and had raised a family with that common law partner, told the team that she was having a relationship with her previous husband and was proposing to leave her common law partner for him. Was this OK? The controversy was over how to apply the commandment "You shall not commit adultery." Some judged the situation as all wrong; others were relieved that she was returning to the original "proper" husband. Still others thought that she should remain true to the common law husband who was of the longest duration and the father of her children.

In the end light came when the story of Jesus and the woman found in adultery was taken to interpret the Old Testament law. The conclusion was that she was free without condemnation to step out into whatever future she chose, so long as she turned at this point from further sin and sought the best circumstances for her children. The Jesus way seems always to apply the law with the maximum possible amount of love and grace.

Now this simple Gospel hermeneutic is sometimes rejected, mainly on two fronts. First there are those who claim that it reduces the authority of Scripture, and then there are those who claim that it limits the application of Scripture today. Both objections misunderstand or misrepresent the method. There is no suggestion whatever that any part of Scripture is less than authoritative. All that is being proposed is that a particular part of Scripture, namely the accounts of the incarnation, is used as the means of interpreting the rest.

The alternative is some other hermeneutic by which themes or doctrines are extracted or systematically explored by the (often hidden) inclination of the theologian. A self-confessed bias to interpreting the Scriptures via the incarnation of Jesus seems highly preferable!

The claim that the Gospels are less than adequate for the interpretation of all other biblical truth for today may seem plausible at first. Usually the point is made that they carry no developed teaching on salvation, the Holy Spirit and the church, because they end with the cross and resurrection. Pentecost and the rest waits for the Book of Acts.

But all these themes are, and indeed must be, embryonic in the Gospels if the incarnation and revelation of God in Christ are complete. Of course the rest of the New Testament is essential for reflecting on and applying the incarnation, the cross, the resurrection and the ascension to the church and to the work of the kingdom today. But this is not contradicted or weakened by interpreting and understanding what is being said in the light of the Gospels. Rather it ensures that we follow the same process as the New Testament writers themselves must have followed as they preached and applied the good news in every situation they entered, using the Old Testament Scriptures as their resource, and the good news about Jesus as their means of understanding and applying them.

CHAPTER 12

RELEASING RESOURCES

Prayer

Prayer is fundamental to the release of resources for church planting, and is itself therefore the primary resource. When Jesus sent out the seventy in those early preparational teams he said to them "Beseech the Lord of the harvest to send out laborers into His harvest" (Lk. 10:2). What applies to human resources clearly applies to physical ones too. He told the same teams to take "no purse, no bag, no shoes", emphasising that the first base of dependency for resources should be God. Jesus taught us to pray both "Thy kingdom come," and "Give us each day our daily bread" (Lk. 11:2–3).

The prophesied culmination of the breakthrough of the kingdom in a generation in John's Revelation, places great emphasis on the mix of "the prayers of the saints" with incense of worship ascending before the throne of God. Then the fire is poured out on the earth. While the primary reference of fire is the outpouring of the Holy Spirit, the progress of the kingdom in Jesus' ministry and in the Old Testament preparation was always accompanied by physical as well as spiritual provision.

The psalmist is unequivocal: "Unless the Lord builds the house, they labor in vain who build it" (Ps. 127:1).

If our church planting is to be a success, then our number one objective in the provision of resources must be to mobilise prayer. The early apostles saw that utterly clearly as they awaited the coming of the Spirit at Pentecost "with one mind, ...continually devoting themselves to prayer" (Acts 1:14). This continual devotion to prayer needs to be the basic framework out of which the church planting team functions.

We have already looked at the spiritual warfare aspects of prayer which are so integral to the process of breakthrough in church planting. The background of faithful prayer for general needs, of supplication over specific identified areas, of intercession to overcome in particularly intransigent situations, all interspersed with thanksgiving for what God has done – and what he is going to do – must be the stronghold in God from which the spiritual battle is fought.

These different aspects of prayer need to be expressed through the regular prayer life of the team. In order to leave plenty of time for front line evangelism, we have found it best to follow Jesus' example of a framework of early morning and late night praying, with occasional seasons of prayer. We tend to go for weekly morning prayer times from say 6.30-8.30 am, a late night time from say 10.30 pm -12.30 am with monthly half-nights and nights of prayer and periods of prayer and fasting where the team puts aside a day or two at a time for concentrated prayer every two or three months.

Which particular programme of prayer is suitable will depend on the stage of maturity and progress of the team's life. These suggestions may seem demanding to some. Others will be only too aware of how poorly they compare with the standard practice of teams in those parts of the world where the greatest growth and provision is taking place. In many such places hundreds or thousands meet to pray every single morning from 5.00 am onwards. The key is to decide with the team and the Holy Spirit together what is possible and appropriate at the contemporary point; not to aim too high or too low and to avoid legalism and condemnation. Better to have a willing few than a pressurised or resentful bunch!

It is important and encouraging to support this team prayer by the build up of as wide a prayer support base as possible. Praying friends and relatives of the planters themselves become the first obvious line of added support. We have found over the years that a smallish list of committed supporters, who welcome being sent a daily prayer diary updated every few months, and who can be contacted at times of particular need, is much more important than a wide net of vaguely interested folk receiving an annual (or more frequent) prayer letter which is rarely seriously read or acted on. Added to this, several totally committed prayer warriors who will take on the situation as a part - or even full-time job (the sort of challenge that elderly or temporarily restricted Christian workers would rise to) provide an excellent prayer position from which to operate.

The rising tide of prayer which is making itself felt in many parts of the world also means that it is currently possible to plug into an increasing number of prayer networks to multiply and extend the amount of prayer cover. This rising tide is multiplying full-time prayer teams in various bases around the world too. When church-planting work multiplies as it has in Ichthus, it becomes a real possibility to set up such a base which can then be a twenty-four-hour resource for prayer. We are currently embarking on such a project and already feel the benefit of it. James summarises the whole point here: "The effective prayer of a righteous man can accomplish much. Elijah was a man with a nature like ours, and he prayed earnestly that it might not rain; and it did not rain ... And he prayed again, and the sky poured rain, and the earth produced its fruit" (Jas. 5:16–18).

Finances

The whole purpose of church planting is to make way for the kingdom of God, and the church is God's agent of the kingdom on the earth. Jesus made it clear that it was exceedingly difficult for rich people to enter this kingdom:

"How hard it will be for those who are wealthy to enter the kingdom of God!" (Mk. 10:23). Wealthy people tend to trust in their riches to provide the power to do things. It is one of the signs of a generation of materialism in the Western world that we rely on the availability of finances to make it possible to take action for God.

Now let me say before we go any further that it is essential to do God's work responsibly, and not casually or with a slipshod attitude. King David emphasised the need for a serious attitude to the service of God when after he had sinned and numbered Israel he said to Araunah, who had offered him land and materials for nothing, "No, but I will surely buy it from you for a price, for I will not offer burnt offerings to the Lord my God which cost me nothing" (2 Sam. 24:24). The issue is not that we shouldn't take our financial responsibilities seriously, but that we should understand that money doesn't provide the resources for God's work. Rather God provides the money that provides the resources. This is the only way to make sense of Jesus' statement about the widow's gift into the temple treasury: "Truly I say to you, this poor widow put in more than all the contributors to the treasury; for they all put in out of their surplus, but she, out of her poverty, put in all she owned, all she had to live on" (Mk. 12:43–44). If this lady gave more than them all, then we can see the radical reversal Jesus makes when we compare his heavenly economics with our earthly ones. The provision of resources doesn't depend on the size of the gift, but the spirit and cost with which it is given. This is because the way to increase funds is to give from the heart: "Give, and it will be given to you; good measure, pressed down, shaken together, running over, they will pour into your lap. For whatever measure you deal out to others, it will be dealt to you in return" (Lk. 6:38).

Materialism is an obstacle to the kingdom and prevents genuine resources being provided in at least two ways. First, it limits our vision and planning to what we know is financially available. This may seem fine if you have lots of funds or rich backers. But it is an enormous problem really because a work could be done entirely without God on that basis.

Second, the opposite side of materialism is the poverty spirit which assumes that we will never have enough money. We always have a pinched and fearful attitude to the work of God, and we simply can't break through unbelief and believe God's promises. Yet it is faith in God's promises that is the key. Once again Jesus is crystal clear: "Man shall not live on bread alone, but on every word that proceeds out of the mouth of God" (Mt. 4:4).

Pioneer church-planting is by definition an area of work for which resources are not generally available within the church. Responsible church life generates funds as people give from the heart. But pioneer church-planting situations don't have churches in them yet. So no funds are generated. We have to take our responsibilities seriously, attend to the quality of our trust in God, develop a giving attitude, and God will find a way to provide the resources.

Once these principles are in place, God is not limited to just one way of working. It is my conviction that the exercise of the gift of faith as a means of provision is particularly appropriate to the task of church planting. More of that shortly. But it is not the only way God can provide for us.

First we may be salaried, and the expenses paid for by financially sound backers. In this case the spiritual exercise and heavenly economics will be practised mainly by those established churches or trusts that have heard God's call to facilitate others into church planting. This has the benefit of taking pressure off the worker who can devote his or her energies to the task of planting. It has the danger, for which the worker must be alert, of taking responsibility away from us. The board or leadership providing the money might be fleshly materialists. We need to look at that and make sure that we are at least submitting those funds to God and doing the work under his guidance and leading, and not just because funds are available. This is true of all means of provision where the primary responsibility for provision is not in the workers' hands. However, many boards and leaderships will likely be even more spiritually aware and responsible than we are, in which case they will be a good check on our own materialistic tendencies.

Then there is the sponsorship method. This method seeks supporters who will undertake to provide a part of the budgeted necessary income to support workers and the work on the ground. Once again it takes pressure off the workers by giving a regular source of income. With the same qualifications as the salary method, it has the advantage again of taking pressure off the church planters, at least once sufficient sponsors have been found. It does have the disadvantage that it is necessary to go out seeking the sponsorship for yourself or your work, unless people are willing to volunteer to provide this help as a spiritual gift to the body. We need more people to see the need for this and prayerfully to solicit sponsorship on other people's behalf. This avoids self-promotion and the relationship difficulties involved in seemingly promoting one's own cause.

Another way is the tent-making method, so called because of Paul's practice of providing for his needs or supplementing his gift income by practising his skills at tent-making. Workers find some skill or employment that will release funds to supplement their sponsorship income or combine together with the direct gifts they pray in as they exercise a gift of faith. In Ichthus, the church planting has been sufficiently successful for the movement as a whole to make the pump priming finances available for new church-planting work on the ground. In the case of the workers in the team, however, they either pay for themselves as part of the Network training process, or else a relatively small gift of half or less of what it really costs to live and engage in Christian work is made available by the movement on a monthly basis when possible. The rest of the income is provided by a combination of tent-making and the exercise of the gift of faith. People do part-time teaching, act as security personnel, take in paying guests, take in proof reading, drive, mend roofs, take on painting and decorating and so on, as and when necessary.

A further way of minimising expenses and building team life in a quite intense way is to practise some form of corporate living. Jesus and his disciples did this some of the time as they travelled together, keeping a common purse and handling some or all of their expenses corporately. Some church planters have committed themselves completely to this model and it is certainly a viable alternative. In our experience it carries some difficulties for recognising and promoting the family unit and individual responsibility, but it is an important and highly team building alternative particularly appropriate at some stages of life and for some people. There are many alternative versions of corporate living that can be experimented with. Sue and I have only lived alone, or just with our two sons, for two brief periods amounting to about eighteen months in all throughout more than twenty years of marriage. This has been good for us, although we certainly don't say it is the only way to live!

In the end, however, it is extremely difficult to engage in pioneer church planting without applying the spiritual gift of faith to the provision of resources. This is the only sure way of raising the necessary financial resources for work which does not have any basis for provision because it does not yet exist.

There are a number of things to say about this. First, in the kind of Christian climate where Calvinism has been dominant, it is necessary to point out that there is an important difference between the faith without which it is impossible to please God, and the gift of faith. Some forms of Calvinism have suggested that the faith to believe is itself a gift. This is based on a mistaken exegesis of Ephesians 2. Instead of understanding that it is "grace" which is the gift of God, it has been wrongly thought that it is "faith" which is the gift of God: "For by grace you have been saved through faith; and that not of yourselves, it is the gift of God; not as a result of works, that no one should boast" (Eph. 2:8–9). This mistaken teaching goes on to say that faith, unless God's gift, would be a work! But faith is simply the mechanism through which we receive the gift of God's grace and it is sin not to apply it! If it was itself the gift of God then God would be entirely unjust to hold us responsible as sinners for not exercising it! Paul could not possibly go on to say "whatever is not from faith is sin" (Rom. 14:23).

No, there is a crucial distinction between this general faith that God requires of us, and a special, supernatural gift of faith that God gives to supplement our faith and move us into realms of supernatural provision. It is not sin to fail to exercise this gift, but it is available to us, and is especially helpful in the context of apostolic work. "Now there are varieties of gifts, but the same Spirit ... For to one is given the word of wisdom through the Spirit, and to another the word of knowledge according to the same Spirit; to another faith by the same Spirit ..." (1 Cor. 12:4, 8–9). It was surely this gift which the Lord was encouraging the early disciples to exercise when he sent them out without purse or bag, denying them even the possibility of greeting passers by, let alone begging from them!

It was this gift that was so remarkably demonstrated in more recent pioneer disciples. It was the means by which George Muller provided so famously for his orphans, and which earned Rees Howells the reputation that if he looked over the wall of a Swansea property the owner might as well move out because God would get him out otherwise!

This gift is not, of course, restricted to faith for financial provision, and is extremely relevant to breaking through the apparent impossibilities of church planting in new lands and localities, to the multiplication of converts, the rapid growth and development of leadership and dealing with obstacles generally. In my own experience it has been a main source of financial provision for the best part of twenty years.

This gift of faith then, is the supernatural supplement to the faith which Abraham had, which trusts God, and is counted to us as righteousness. "Faith was reckoned to Abraham as righteousness" (Rom. 4:9). This Abraham-type faith is the "mustard seed" which provides the way for God to act supernaturally on our behalf. Jesus spoke of this kind of faith on several occasions. When his disciples were unable to cast the demon out of a boy, he spoke of the littleness of their faith and said "For truly I say to you, if you have faith as a mustard seed, you shall say to this mountain, 'Move from here to there,' and it shall move; and nothing shall be impossible to you" (Mat. 17:20). Yet we can all think of situations when we know that we do have the mustard seed of saving faith, but we cannot move the mountain. There is even still something to connect to. It is the gift of faith that we need.

I have experienced this tangibly when it comes to healing. I have been so much a part of the Western world and its intellectual pride and unbelief when it comes to physical healing that I have often experienced the retreat of the tide of faith in the face of physical healing needs. But on significant occasions, instead of the tide of faith going out, the reverse has happened. Onto my mustard seed of faith God has supernaturally added his faith, a gift of faith. Then the tide has come in and the need met, the person healed. I am quite sure this experience of the gift of faith for healing has been preceded in my case by breakthrough in the area of financial resources. I am increasingly clear as to how it works. As we learn to trust him, Jesus reaches out to us with the gift of faith, saying, as he said to his first disciples, "Have faith in God," or a better translation, "Have the faith of God" (Mk. 11:22). This is the gift of faith, the "faith of God".

Jesus goes on to make it clear that to those who do not doubt God in the deep structure of their hearts will be granted such a gift of faith that it will be possible to believe that the requests are already received, and then the answer will certainly be granted:

> Truly I say to you, whoever says to this mountain, 'Be taken up and cast into the sea,' and does not doubt in his heart, but believes that what he says is going to happen, it shall be granted him. Therefore I say to you, all things for which you pray and ask, believe that you have received them, and they shall be granted you (Mk 11:23–24).

Now this mustn't be some hoping against hope, easy-believism. If the work of God, and the provision for daily living of God's servant and his family are at stake, this must be responsible faith for sure. God first challenged me to this kind of faith for finances in my late teens, long before I was in church-planting work. I had been reading of George Muller, Rees Howells, C T Studd and others with extraordinary testimonies of God's supernatural provision. I was due to spend a few weeks helping a children's evangelist run some summer holiday clubs. It involved travelling away from home, and as I had little money I decided to experiment with the gift of faith. So I deliberately set out without the resources to accomplish the trip. I had an ancient car, and no money for petrol for the return journey, or any keep during the time away. Nothing was at stake save my own pride and understanding of God's call. In a wonderful way God provided everything I needed, without me making my needs known to anyone or, indeed, letting anyone know of the experiment I was engaging in.

Some years later when the opportunity came to be involved in pioneer evangelism and then church planting, living by faith seemed the obvious, and indeed was the only available, method of provision. Practised responsibly on an individual basis it involves very close scrutiny of day-to-day expenses so that specific faith can be exercised. Again and again God finds a way to provide. At first when expenses are low, perhaps just for a single person, it involves trusting God for relatively small sums. Gradually, however, as God increases the gift of faith, much larger sums are involved as the needs of family and of whole work projects develop. As the sums of money and the extent of needs grow it becomes harder to know the detail of need and expense. But in order for the gift to operate properly, in my experience, it is necessary to take steps to make sure that the needs continue to be clearly known. As teams and organisations grow then careful accounting with regular presentation of income and expenditure is imperative so that the gift of faith can still be adequately exercised. Otherwise we can move from faith to presumption and become casual or take the whole process for granted. It may well be that large works with huge budgets can operate in this way as long as accounts staff understand the principles involved and intercessors with the gift of faith are found who can give themselves to maintaining the flow of finances required.

None of this need imply that the gift of faith cannot be used in conjunction with other ways of releasing resources for church-planting work. The gift of faith is at least partially reliant on external factors other than God! It requires people with finances, small or great, to be listening for God's prompting to give. It assumes a social and political environment in which people are allowed to give to full time Christian work and so on. Tent-making in particular is a responsible back up.

Buildings

At risk of emphasising the obvious, it must be remembered that churches are built out of living stones not physical ones. Churches are communities of people with whom God lives, not religious buildings that God lives in! Of course we may accept that a secondary, derivative meaning of the word 'church' is the building that houses the church. But it is not a matter we can afford to be vague or casual about. Jesus and Stephen both regarded the distinction as one worth dying for! We have already noted in our opening chapter that Jesus builds church out of people: "And I also say to you that you are Peter, and upon this rock I will build My church" (Mat. 16:18).

John describes Jesus' conversation with the Jews after the first cleansing of the temple. "'Destroy this temple, and in three days I will raise it up.' The Jews therefore said, 'It took forty-six years to build this temple, and will You raise it up in three days?' But he was speaking of the temple of His body" (Jn. 2:19–21). Paul later declares to the Corinthian church, "Do you not know that you are a temple of God, and that the Spirit of God dwells in you?" (1 Cor. 3:16).

Stephen was stoned for his unequivocal statements about the nature of God's dwelling place when he said, "The Most High does not dwell in houses made by human hands; as the prophet says: 'Heaven is My throne, and earth is the footstool of My feet; what kind of house will you build for Me?' says the Lord; 'Or what place is there for my repose?'" (Acts 7:48–49). Peter brings the clear answer to the prophet's question in his epistle, and invites us to come to Jesus

> "as to a living stone, rejected by men, but choice and precious in the sight of God, you also, as living stones, are being built up as a spiritual house" (1 Pet. 2:4–5).

Paul concludes for us, writing to the Ephesians:

> You are no longer strangers and aliens, but you are fellow-citizens with the saints, and are of God's household, having been built upon the foundation of the apostles and prophets, Christ Jesus Himself being the corner stone, in whom the whole building, being fitted together is growing into a holy temple in the Lord; in whom you also are being built together into a dwelling of God in the Spirit (Eph. 2:19–22).

Church planters are seeking humbly to be the channel, the vehicle, through which and out of which Jesus builds his church. All our ideas and preconceptions of suitable meeting places, and "church buildings" must be submitted to this primary reality of church. For us there can be no "sanctuaries" and holy artifacts. Not if they limit the growth and expression of the body of Christ. Places where you must whisper on tiptoe and objects that you can't ordinarily move, are immediately suspect!

In our experience, places in which people feel at home are the best buildings to start church planting in. Our preacher last night got it exactly right for the inner city when he paraphrased the Authorised Version of John's words, "And the Word became flesh and tabernacled among us," as, "The Word became flesh and council-flatted among us." But while this is often the best place to start, it mustn't be allowed to limit growth. When Ichthus began meeting in Roger and Faith Forster's front room, there were those who felt it would be growth enough to demolish a wall into the study so that we could all fit in nicely. Instead we moved to a Senior Citizens' club room which held up to forty people. From there we went to the local Quaker meeting house, on to a Lutheran Church and afterwards to the comprehensive school hall. In the meantime we saw the strengths of the home group and so continued the regular home-group meetings as the basic building block of church life. We saw too the benefit of a local congregation meeting and being publicly in a locally definable area. So as we grew we reached out to plant more and more of such congregations, while celebrating regularly on the larger scale in the school or other similar suitable buildings as we grew and multiplied celebrations as well. The local congregations found the most suitable public premises available. These ranged from community centres, pub function rooms, leisure centre rooms, night clubs, dance halls and schools to church buildings themselves.

In inner-city areas especially, the decline of living church life and church-going has left many empty church buildings. Some older established church and mission groupings have been wonderful in making buildings easily available at low or no rent. Others have been less helpful and insisted on market rents or market freehold selling prices. We would make the plea for those responsible for such buildings to let the hard work and prayers of past generations serve the new church-planting teams of this generation as much as possible.

When all else fails, it could be necessary to build, but in the main, building large church premises needs to be limited to situations of necessity, and then to be multi-purpose, where the building serves the church across a wide area in as many ways as possible in any one day. Otherwise finances are better spent in facilitating people!

One final point on the subject of buildings relates to the need to cleanse and release buildings from the spiritual atmosphere and authority under which they have often been used. There is no doubt that places can become contaminated by wrong practices and wrong uses. John speaks in the Revelation of how the city of Babylon "has become a dwelling place of demons and a prison of every unclean spirit" (Rev. 18:2). It follows that buildings which have been submitted to the authority of Babylon – and all it stands for in terms of injustice, immorality, false religion and occult practice – can be affected in a negative way and need submitting to the lordship and worship of Jesus and cleansing by the power of his blood. Some buildings, because of the nature of the authority they come under, may well best be left alone altogether as the Holy Spirit indicates.

CHAPTER 13

TEAM BUILDING

Team building is the very nature and substance of church. Church is not first and foremost a structure, let alone an institution. Rather it is a living body. Church is not something that people belong to, it is something that Christians *are*.

We saw in our first chapter that Jesus taught specifically about church on two occasions. The first outlined for us what church is and the second taught us how to preserve it. We shall return to this second emphasis shortly. It was in this context that Jesus made his famous statement: "For where two or three have gathered together in My name, there I am in their midst" (Mt. 18:20). Church is this essential basic relationship which Jesus inhabits. Paul expressed it succinctly when he said, "Now you are Christ's body, and individually members of it" (1 Cor. 12:27). This togetherness between individuals in Christ transcends all the fundamental human barriers of race, class and gender: "There is neither Jew nor Greek, there is neither slave nor free man, there is neither male nor female; for you are all one in Christ Jesus" (Gal. 3:28).

Togetherness between men and women from every tribe, tongue and nation is the consequence of the gospel and the culmination of God's plans in history. As the sixth seal of the scroll of God's plans for mankind is broken in John's Revelation, he looked "and behold, a great multitude, which no one could count, from every nation and all tribes and peoples and tongues, standing before the throne and before the Lamb" (Rev. 7:9). The desire at the very heart of the Trinity, revealed before the cross, as Jesus laboured in prayer, sums it all up. "And the glory which Thou hast given Me I have given to them; that they may be one, just as We are one; I in them, and Thou in Me, that they may be perfected in unity, that the world may know that Thou didst send Me, and didst love them, even as Thou didst love me" (Jn 17:22–23).

Peter, to whom the first revelation of the nature of church was given, clearly saw the radical implications. This church, built on the revelation of Jesus, was no less than a completely new society, superseding and fulfilling the Jews' special destiny and purpose. As he explained it to the church in his epistle: "You are a chosen race, a royal priesthood, a holy nation, a people for God's own possession, that you may proclaim the excellencies of Him who has called you out of darkness into His marvellous light; for you once were not a people, but now you are the people of God ..." (1 Pet. 2:9–10).

This holy nation is fundamental to God's strategy in the history of mankind. It gives him a stronghold in the occupied territory of his creation from which he can reach out in partnership with his people and finally overcome his enemies. At the same time it is also the very taste of victory itself as the relationships of eternity are forged and enjoyed. Paul explains to the Ephesians:

> You are no longer strangers and aliens, but you are fellow–citizens with the saints, and are of God's household, having been built upon the foundation of the apostles and prophets, Christ Jesus Himself being the corner stone, in whom the whole building, being fitted together is growing into a holy temple in the Lord; in whom you also are being built together into a dwelling of God in the Spirit" (Eph. 2:19–22).

We will come back to these dual aspects of church – the practical work task and the joy that is an end in itself – in a few moments. Just now I want to emphasise the practical role of the church in manifesting the image of God through its togetherness in a way which it would be quite impossible for the individual parts to do. This need for interdependence between people if God's image is to be seen has been emphasised by God from the word go – when God first made mankind in his image: "In the image of God He created him; male and female He created them" (Gen. 1:27); when the first man was alone, God said, "It is not good for the man to be alone; I will make him a helper suitable for him" (Gen. 2:18). This first team relationship set the norm for human life; a norm which Jesus reiterated clearly when he came: "For this cause a man shall leave his father and his mother, and shall cleave to his wife; and they shall become one flesh" (Gen 2:24, Mt. 19:5).

Throughout the history of mankind marriage has been, and remains, a fundamental building block for God's corporate purposes for the human race. His image is seen through a man and a woman committed to each other in love, and committed to the world in the communication of the person and purpose of God. This principle is extended in the team life of the body of Christ to include what Paul calls the many-sided wisdom of God, as the glorious mix of race, culture, disposition and social background is added to the already potent solution of male and female. This combination is so powerful as to reveal the image of God to the principalities and powers: "That the manifold wisdom of God might now be made known through the church to the rulers and the authorities in the heavenly places" (Eph. 3:10).

There are issues to be careful of in relating marriage to the relationships of the body of Christ, which we shall also look at later in this chapter, but its place in revealing the interdependence of individuals under God is clear, as is its ongoing role within the church. When it is working well, Paul says that it reveals not only the image of God, but also his intended relationship with his body as the bride to a husband.

The interdependence of man and wife is what God himself looks for with his people.

Because team is what God is after, what he wants to reproduce, it should be unequivocally clear by now that no Christian leadership, let alone the leadership of the church or a church-planting team, can ignore or neglect the building up of team life. Even the Old Testament biblical models of leadership, whom we sometimes think of as towering individuals leading in lone splendour, actually worked in team. Moses, for example, worked with Miriam and Aaron and had Joshua in close relationship, training on the job. Elijah had Elisha and the relationships of the prophetic schools. But above all it was the Lord himself in whom "it was the Father's good pleasure for all the fulness to dwell" (Col. 1:19) who demonstrated the Father's absolute commitment to team life when he began his ministry by calling together the twelve and by sending them out in teams as they grew and were trained as the leaders of the embryonic church.

One of the most poignant recollections of the power of team life to make known the image of God and to break demonic strongholds occurred with a young semi-punk teenager in the early days of our Ichthus church planting. Broken up by years of chaotic home life, suffering the physical oppressions that are so often the result of generations of inner-city underclass life outside any living contact with the church of Jesus, he seemed an unlikely candidate for rapid conversion. He'd hardly had time to get to know the bunch of us at work on the streets before he was pressing to give his life to Jesus. I remember trying to argue him out of making a commitment too quickly. But he was adamant. "There's nothing special about you guys for a start," he said. "But you've got love. And seeing as how you're nothing special, it don't come from you. So it must come from God. And I want it."

That's the task of the church of Jesus. To shine the light of his love through the interface of our personalities in relationship together in him. Then the world will know. Then the devil will have to let go. The light will outshine the satanic darkness. Therefore we need to make deliberate conscious efforts to build team life throughout every level of church life and all the structures of our church planting. This is what Jesus did, as we shall now see.

Jesus' team-building principles

> And He went up to the mountain and summoned those whom He Himself wanted, and they came to Him. And He appointed twelve, that they might be with Him, and that He might send them out to preach, and to have authority to cast out the demons. And He appointed the twelve: Simon (to whom He gave the name Peter); and James, the son of Zebedee, and John the brother of James (to them He gave the name Boanerges, which means, 'Sons of Thunder'); and Andrew, and Philip, and Bartholomew, and Matthew, and Thomas, and James the son of Alphaeus, and Thaddaeus, and Simon the Cananaean; and Judas Iscariot, who also betrayed Him (Mk 3:13–19).

The first thing to note about Jesus' way of team building is that he called to him those whom he wanted. So one of the big reasons for building team at all, was that he wanted their company. This care that Jesus had for his team, and which he continues to have for those who corporately follow his call, is a powerful theme in the Gospels, and in the Old Testament relationships that go before them. Jesus prays for them in intimate terms before the cross. "I ask on their behalf: I do not ask on behalf of the world, but of those whom Thou hast given Me" (Jn 17:9). Isaiah speaks of God's servants: "Do not fear, for I have redeemed you; I have called you by name; you are Mine!" (Is. 43:1). This care for his team was fundamental to the loyalty and commitment that held them together. So it will be with our contemporary teams. The church planter needs to choose a team, and to choose to love them and care for them in Jesus' name.

Now of course as churches grow, and indeed in the case of some peers in team life from the start, not all relationships in our teams will be 'chosen'. Some will be what we could call 'givens', ie other people's chosens whom we end up working with because we responded to the invitation of the person or people who also chose them. If team is going to work in these situations then we will need to decide to choose the 'givens'. This is the very nature of Jesus' kind of *agape* loving. It is not based originally on liking or preference, but on choice. He has let this kind of love loose by the original choice of us humans, despite our sinfulness. Now it is available for us to receive and love with, through the cross and the present Holy Spirit.

This choice to love is essential to the team life that is at the heart of the body of Christ. Nothing else can break down the walls and barriers that race, class, sex and social background, (all exacerbated by sin) have thrown up between human beings. This barrier-breaking love is what the church exists to experience and let loose. We shouldn't be surprised therefore when we find ourselves put together with people who seem peculiarly difficult to get along with, or who find it hard to get along with us! This is very obvious from Jesus' own choice of disciples, who were carefully chosen and wanted by the Lord, and yet had enormous potential for disagreement and difficulty in relationship.

It is very important to note at this stage, that although Jesus chose a group of people who were in many ways similar: all male, all Jews, all free men (what is technically called an 'homogeneous' group) there were actually outstanding differences between them. Simon the Zealot belonged to a political activist party which advocated the use of violence, particularly against the tax collectors for the Romans. Matthew collected taxes for the Romans! Simon Barjona was renamed Peter the rock, when he was manifestly unstable and like shifting sand to begin with. It seems unlikely therefore that James and John, the Sons of Thunder, were among the shyest quietest types of men! As they learned to love and make room for each other, they were led by Jesus to encounter and receive the Samaritan woman, the Roman Centurion and his slave, to name but a few.

As we learn to live together in team life, our good news will grow in authenticity and men and women will want to join our kingdom lifestyle and become Christians themselves.

Church-planting team life needs to be a statement of the power and reality of the gospel. The disciples were a disparate group, yet homogeneous at a starting level. As we move out into working-class housing areas, Muslim cities, or wherever, we will begin to build teams which have a growing experience of homogeneity. We must never forget, however, that Jesus means these as a starting point for the adventure of seeing God's kingdom come, where all kinds, types and shapes of Christians are bound together in love. These groups are technically called 'heterogeneous' groups. Ultimately they must be our goal.

As well as choosing his team to be with him, and shaping them into the style and relationship of the kingdom of heaven, Jesus called his team together to preach the gospel and cast out demons. It is vital to keep a healthy tension alive in team life, between being together for its own sake in demonstration and consummation of God's kind of loving on the one hand, and working together in the work of the kingdom on the other. It is helpful to see these two things as kingdom being and kingdom doing. Kingdom being alone leads to stagnation and purposelessness in the end, and needs action to give point and purpose to team relationship. A body, after all, exists for action, not for fitness for its own sake. That is no more than narcissism. We need to beware the desire to produce perfect bodies for their own sake.

The Lord spoke to us in the earliest days of Ichthus from the Authorised Version translation of Isaiah's words, "They shall see eye to eye, when the Lord shall bring again Zion" (Is. 52:8). We understood clearly that this was not an eyeball to eyeball inward looking, but rather an alongside, eye to eye in parallel kind of seeing as we go forward together in the work of the gospel. This, we saw, was the early church's "all things in common" (Acts 2:44).

Team life in action requires the kind of team leadership that involves the team leader on the ground, in action in evangelism with the rest of the team, just like Jesus was. But at the same time, team life must be more than activism. If Jesus wants us together with him, then team life requires time in his presence, in love and worship of him, exposing our lives to his word and input, communing together in prayer and mutual support. Paul makes it clear that we are to meet together with Christ in the Holy Spirit "speaking to one another in psalms and hymns and spiritual songs, singing and making melody with your heart to the Lord; always giving thanks for all things ..." (Eph. 5:19–20). James tells us, "Confess your sins to one another, and pray for one another" (Jas. 5:16). Team life needs to be scheduled around times of fellowship together in the Holy Spirit like this. We have found it essential to spend several hours a week together in this way, and where possible in mission situations an hour or more together like this every day.

However, Jesus also gave time for social interaction together and for one-to-one or one-to-three relationships. He gave time while travelling to communicate at leisure with the disciples. He selected special times to be with various disciples on the mountain, in the garden, out on the lake and so on. He planned times of rest and visits to weddings and parties. Of course it wasn't possible to compartmentalise these different aspects of team life rigidly. But we need to understand the importance of them all and work to give weight to them. We have found it helpful to arrange love feasts where we can relax over a meal and then break bread together; to arrange times away walking in the hills; to encourage those who are so inclined to play sports or enjoy shared interests together. Of course we are at war, so we won't be able to over-balance into too much rest or relaxation if we keep Christ's way in front of us. But we will make a priority to be together for its own sake from time to time.

I experienced a quantum leap in team life with several teams I was leading when I booked in regular time, say an hour or so every three weeks, to sit down with individual team members on a one-to-one basis, specifically to talk and share spontaneously on issues of personal concern whether related to the work of the kingdom, personal development or relationships. At first there was a slight awkwardness with some of these encounters, but frankness together in the Holy Spirit has taken us forward. This is surely what Paul has in view when he says, "Speaking the truth in love, we are to grow up in all aspects into Him, who is the head, even Christ..." (Eph. 4:15). If we don't give time to speak together these things won't happen, whatever our ministry gift may be!

At this point it may be helpful to make a few observations about marriage in the context of team life. There are two main issues here. The first is that Christian marriage, as we have already observed, is the most fundamental of team relationships. Therefore those who are married must be sure to give priority to their marriage relationship and any children who belong to it, without feeling awkward about it. Good marriage relationships, with the sexual glue that uniquely strengthens them, make a wonderful contribution to team building. This is true whether or not both parties are in the wider team. Strong and fulfilling marriages produce balanced and reliable team members who can relate across the sexes healthily because they become increasingly gender compatible with both sexes, and have no tendency to relate with their team colleagues in a sexual way. This is very positive for single team members and a far cry from the way things often operate in the world or in churches and teams that the world's way has penetrated.

There is, however, a second important issue to be aware of in connection with marriage in team life, particularly where both partners are in the same team. It is important for those partners not to use their marriage relationship, either consciously or unconsciously, to the disadvantage of the other team members. This requires growing maturity to get right, but it is possible to do so. Married couples must not become an inner bastion of decision-making partnership or exclusive relationship when the team is together. My wife Sue and I have found it helpful not to call one another by our private terms of endearment or refer too often to the inside knowledge that we are bound to have. Rather we try to use the strength of our private lives to enable each other to relate meaningfully to the other members of the team. In our experience, all teams require a leader, including leadership teams. A marriage partnership needs to be exercised with great care in the team context, therefore, if the other team members and relationships are not to be excluded or robbed of their proper role and value.

This is not to say that we should be afraid of special relationships in team life. Friendship is not something to be afraid of if it is in the Spirit. Jesus called his disciples 'friends' (Jn. 15:14). John the apostle referred to himself as the "disciple whom Jesus loved" (Jn. 21:20). Jesus clearly developed particular relationships with Peter, James and John; Mary, Martha and Lazarus, Mary Magdalene and so on. David and Jonathan provide a clear Old Testament precedent for this, together with the key to staying in the Spirit and not falling into the flesh: "Jonathan said to David, '... we have sworn to each other in the name of the Lord, saying, "The Lord will be between me and you, and between my descendants and your descendants forever"'" (1 Sam. 20:42).

If we welcome the Holy Spirit very seriously into all aspects of our relationships and submit them wholeheartedly to him, they will be given and taken only as he leads. These different, unique relationships between various members of a team will occasionally throw up problems as irritations rise to the surface and jealousy, manipulation and misunderstanding occur. These are not things to be afraid of, but should be faced and prayed and talked through, so that the very complications that occur can become the channels through which the Holy Spirit flows.

It remains to face the reality of what to do when things go wrong in team life. It is my conviction that we can be saved from the compounded, long-lasting and sometimes incurable problems associated with team relationships if we follow a few simple guidelines. This is not to say they are simple to follow. In fact they involve frequent, even daily, dying! But who said that following Jesus meant anything less? Indeed, He said that daily death, the loss of our own lives whether by life or death, was precisely how we would find them: "And He was saying to them all, 'If anyone wishes to come after Me, let him deny himself, and take up his cross daily, and follow Me. For whoever wishes to save his life shall lose it, but whoever loses his life for My sake, he is the one who will save it'" (Lk. 9:23–24).

Jesus, as we have already noted several times, spoke of church on two main occasions. The second of these gives us his simple guidance on how to preserve team life. He is straight to the point:

> If your brother sins, go and reprove him in private; if he listens to you, you have won your brother. But if he does not listen to you, take one or two more with you, so that by the mouth of two or three witnesses every fact may be confirmed. And if he refuses to listen to them, tell it to the church; and if he refuses to listen even to the church, let him be to you as a Gentile and a tax-gatherer (Mat. 18:15–17).

Several observations can be made from these verses and those that follow. First, the issue in question here is not a personal matter of a sin against me. Sins like that I'm simply required to forgive. But if there is an ongoing practice of sin – or an ugly weed of sin that is damaging the person who is committing it, or seriously damaging the name of Jesus, outsiders, or other team members – then we need to face the person with it.

Secondly, the issue must be exceedingly serious because I'll need to be ready to make it an issue to take to the whole church in order for them to adjudicate over it if the person won't accept my reproof. I'll even need to be ready to break fellowship in the Holy Spirit over it. So it will need to be something that the Holy Spirit agrees with me in or else it may be me who ends up grieving the Holy Spirit!

Thirdly, my problem with a brother or sister needs to be tackled in prayer and strong spiritual warfare. To me, the significance of the very next verse to the instructions of the Lord we have been looking at, is clear: "Truly I say to you, whatever you shall bind on earth shall have been bound in heaven; and whatever you loose on earth shall have been loosed in heaven" (Mat. 18:18). This verse locates church discipline firmly into the battle with Satan.

Apart from applying these clear instructions, the only other thing to do is humble ourselves as Jesus did. If the issues are not at this level of going to a brother or sister, prepared to break fellowship with them, with the full agreement of the church and the Holy Spirit (so we'll have to be right about this!), then the only thing to do is intercede, love and die! May God help us to do this.

When Jesus was faced with the greatest calumny of his team life (his betrayal by Judas Iscariot), even then he didn't make a public issue of it, but washed his disciples' feet, including Judas', and died: "He said to them, 'Do you know what I have done to you? You call Me Teacher and Lord; and you are right; for so I am. If I then, the Lord and the Teacher, washed your feet, you also ought to wash one another's feet. For I gave you an example that you also should do as I did to you'" (Jn. 13:12–15). This has been the way, by the grace of God, we have tried to head in our team life at Ichthus. The extent to which we have succeeded is seen in the measure of life and power against the enemy we have experienced. This life and power will grow as those relationships go on growing and providing a stronghold for God.

APPENDIX

PERSPECTIVES ON CHURCH PLANTING

by Sandy Millar

Some years ago a friend of mine said something that I have never forgotten. "If the American railroad companies in the 1930s had been interested in the transportation of people", he said, "they'd have bought aeroplanes!" I suppose it struck me particularly forcefully because of what it said about priorities and the adaptability that is required if a vision or purpose is to be recaptured or retained successfully in a world of rapid change.

In the context of church life the questions raised by this train of thought seek answers even more urgently – what are our priorities and what does the church exist for? Inseparable from this and even more important – *Who* does the church exist for? And how are we getting on? Not only that though. Again and again elsewhere in this book the same issues seem to arise – how adaptable are we? Do the structures that were set up to facilitate growth and order, to encourage and set free every member to do the job to which God has called him or her, function properly? Or not? And, if not, what can we do about it?

The figures revealed by the recent Marc Europe survey are well known and they are not encouraging. They show that in this country, from the Church of England alone, we have been losing members at the rate of 1,000 per week for the last 10 years. That is 500,000 people of whom 80% are under the age of 20. It is surely not alarmist to ask how any organisation can afford to be complacent in the face of such facts. The figures themselves come as no real surprise – but they confirm the impression and sense of decline and decay that has contributed to what I believe is the low morale amongst many who comprise the ordinary membership of the Church of England.

Another constituent in the low-morale factor is the perception, not always accurate but sufficiently so to be difficult to counter, that no one seems to know what, if anything, can be suggested by way of remedy. Of course there are exceptions and in recent months some very encouraging signs that there is a growing awareness of the problems. Nevertheless, it is surely no exaggeration to say that the Church of England today is at a cross-roads.

There are, of course, a number of different factors which many would want to point to in the areas of faith, morals and finance, in which agreement may not be easy to reach, either as to the nature of the problem or as to the solution. In the meantime though, it should not take very long for us, as a church, to observe the lessons that are being learned all over the world and, in particular, in the uncontestable, and as far as I know uncontested fact that churches, denominations, groups that are growing significantly all share one common factor – they are "planting" churches.

Peter Wagner, who has made a study of church growth world wide, has been widely quoted with his dictum: "the most effective means of growing churches today is planting churches." I'm not sure if he has said it (but I'm sure he means it!): the *only* effective way to grow churches quickly is to plant churches. The evidence is overwhelming, well researched and covered in various recent books, not all by him, on the subject.

So the reasonable question that follows is this: can the Church of England plant churches? And if the answer given is yes – there have been at the time of writing over 130 church plants of one kind or another in the last 6 years or so in the Church of England – then we may have to rephrase the question. Granted that the Church of England can plant churches, can we plant churches flexibly and quickly enough to respond to what the Spirit of God is doing in Britain today? Put another way: can we encourage the real signs of renewed life that there are and capitalize on the growth that God is undoubtedly sending today in a way that recognizes the challenge that the New Churches have presented to us and enables us to take our place alongside them as partners in the task that we have together. For an answer to this I think we must return to the questions raised a moment ago. What are our real priorities? And how adaptable are we really willing to be?

The point has been made many times in recent years but unhappily is still valid today: the Church of England, in general, is geared to maintenance and not mission. As Eddie Gibbs, another expert in church growth and, with Peter Wagner, also currently in the U.S.A., puts it: "Theological training today prepares us more to be the keeper of an aquarium than a fisher of men." Of course an aquarium needs keeping but unless some attention is given to the fishing aspect it is no wonder that the aquarium suffers and the fish with it.

Jesus told his church to go and make disciples. My belief is that we have lost sight of that command as a priority. It is not just that we're not good at it; it is that we no longer recognize that it is that to which we are called. Making disciples is of course a process. It is not a one-off moment in an individual's life. But the process cannot begin if we're not bringing new people into the church; and is unlikely to begin unless we can agree that it is the top priority now. The proven method of bringing new people into the church is undoubtedly through recognizing and doing church planting. Very strong reasons, it seems to me, are given elsewhere in this book as to both why and how it might be done. My purpose here is to suggest that the same reasons apply, sometimes in different ways and with different emphases, to the Church of England as they do to any New, House or Free Church.

Therefore if it is granted that our priority at this time must be making new disciples, in what ways do the principles that are being applied to other denominations or New Churches apply to the Church of England and in what ways do they differ? And, granted that there may be ways in which they differ, can church planting nevertheless be made to work on a wide scale?

With this I turn from the question of our priorities to the much more contentious issue of whether we have the will to adapt and can help one another through the process. I'd like to look at this under a number of headings.

Parish boundaries

There is a certain irony in the stated aim of the DAWN 2000 (Discipling A Whole Nation) movement to ensure that by the year 2000 there is a living church community within easy reach geographically and ethnically of every 1000 people in the community, for the simple reason that, at the start of the parish system roughly 1000 years ago, that presumably was not just the aim but the achievement of the state church! There was a parish church serving each community and capable of reaching everyone in the community. But in those days communities were based on geography and each church presumably had manageable numbers. Certainly today in urban areas neither of these factors is the same and in some cases the effect of maintaining the old parochial boundaries is demonstrably to give immunity to thousands of people living in them from the opportunity to hear the gospel, as the local church cannot cope.

There is doubtless more than one reason for a church community holding together but in an urban area which has been affected by modern commercial life, with the growth of mobility and separation of individuals from close family roots in a small, old-style community, the most recognizable common factor is friendship. Whether it is a good thing or not, a particular feature about someone living and working in a city like London is often that he (or she) has a circle of friends and relations who will be widely dispersed and whom he sees by arrangement; but he will not expect to be closely involved with neighbours in anything like the way he would have been before the invention of the car, bus or train.

One of the reasons for this is almost certainly that he leaves home at 7 a.m., returning at about 7 p.m. and the news that he hears is more likely to be gained from television or newspapers than from local chat. So he'll know more about what is going on in Accra than two doors away, and he almost certainly won't even know what parish he lives in, let alone feel drawn to the parish church *as* parish church. So he goes to the restaurant he wants to (probably through the recommendation of friends), the shops, the barber and the church he wants to, for the same reasons. If it is true to say that in these circumstances the basis of community has shifted (from geography to friendship) it is important for us in the church to recognize this shift and be capable of adapting quickly to this new situation by being willing to re-draw parish boundaries (both maps and in our thinking) in pencil rather than ink. As Dr. George Carey, the Archbishop of Canterbury, speaking at a recent church-planting conference said, "God must cry when he sees the potential outlets blocked by structure – blocked by inward-looking attitudes." Surely that must be right?

Every recent church report has recognized that the parish is no longer the appropriate geographical area with which to work; (Canon Tiller's report suggested the Deanery as being more practical) but parochial thinking in its literal sense is still deeply embedded in the hearts of many clergy. This is important because if members of a church are being encouraged to bring in new people (which we have just agreed is our priority) the new people are most likely to be drawn from the circle of their friends, who will not necessarily live in any more easily defined area than Greater London – if even that is large enough to cover the diversity!

It is readily seen that the parochial area and way of thinking therefore, whilst good for pastoral care and maintenance, is not for mission. For the new people that are brought by friends will almost certainly all live in different parishes and might be thought, under the "parochial" way of thinking, to be the responsibility of some other church. The only trouble about this is that not only have they not been reached by that other church but, much more importantly, that other church has no real way of reaching them at all, because it has no link with them. Indeed the only Christian link with them is their friend, who doesn't live in the same parish and goes to a different church. So why could we not agree that, for the purposes of mission, there are no helpful geographical boundaries? We are in this together and we must support one another.

Liturgy

The second area in which we must learn to adapt is the requirement that liturgy should be uniform. It seems to me as hard to justify (except on the basis that it is the law and we must not change it) that different types of congregations should have the same liturgy regardless of whether they appreciate it, want it or can cope with it, as it would be to suggest that the same congregation should always have the same liturgy without variation. I freely acknowledge that great strides have been made recently in the provision of variety within the set liturgy but little or no account is taken of those whose longing is for something much less structured, free-er and more adaptable to the sense of occasion at the time of worship. To quote Dr. Carey again:

> Coming from a working class background I know that for the priest to stand there and go over the very long prayer of thanksgiving ... they are far too long for the average working class congregation. Somewhere we need to snip them here and there. Well, we must all work away at that particular problem.

If I could add a comment I would say that I don't think this applies only to an "average working class congregation"! The spirit of this age is for informality and spontaneity and we push water uphill in our attempts to formalize and structure tightly a movement of God's Spirit. Indeed the informality and freshness is part of the great attraction to the New Church movement and we are unwise to ignore it. I know that a willingness to adapt in this area carries with it all the dangers of a sort of self-created congregationalism and I am also aware that such a move is thought to be inconsistent with the values of the Church of England in its search for unity. But unity has never required uniformity and in any event there is already a very great variety of practice within different parish traditions - what have we to lose from a greater variety and freedom in liturgy? I don't think we lose anything – certainly not compared with the opportunities we are currently losing to draw into the kingdom of God people who are mystified, until initiated, (if they stay long enough!) at much of what is said and done in church.

Ordination and training for leadership

A third area in which we need to adapt is in our attitude to ordination and training for leadership. Whilst, for the right person at the right college the opportunity to train for two or three years proves exactly right, there are nevertheless an increasing number of young people for whom such training is quite unsuitable. We have got to be able to recognize gifted people who might not want or be able to cope with an academic emphasis and for whom the pathway to leadership consists much more in the on-the-job training that is being developed so successfully by the New Churches.

Quite apart from that, though, we have got to be able to produce leaders more quickly if we are going to be able to plant churches to keep up with the growth that I believe God is going to send and which there is every reason to believe has already begun. We must return, too, to the New Testament understanding of the priesthood of all believers. There is, of course, a particular calling to full-time Christian leadership; its function is to equip, train, recognize and release the other members of the church in the giftings and callings that God has placed on their life.

Increased number of churches

The fourth area that I think we as the Church of England must face together may require adaption or it may need a total reverse-thrust! The basic philosophy behind church planting is that the *more* "churches" there are in an area (given a sufficient population) the easier and more successful the total effect of all those churches will be. The currently accepted view in the Church of England as a whole, I believe, would be the opposite – viz that the more churches there are the more competition there will be for the same number of souls and hence the harder it will be for each Church. In practice it has been proven that the church-planting view is right. This is partly because with more churches there is a greater amount of prayer, which prepares the way for the spiritual work necessary to bring more people into church; partly because there is a greater variety for people to choose from and to find a spiritual body where they can feel at home (why shouldn't they be able to choose?) and partly, too, because there is a heightened interest within the people of the area caused by the increased number of those who are talking about Christian things. At the time of an effective mission to our area one of the by-products is often that "everyone is talking about it". That can only benefit every church. But I freely admit that the idea of another church starting in the same area can be very threatening; in practice though, providing it is sensitively done, it nearly always proves to be a great blessing.

Our own experiences in church planting have been limited but very rewarding and fruitful. We got the idea from abroad in the first place but we were pushed along by a combination of events as well; the church was full, a curate was ready to move and we had a number of members of the congregation who lived roughly in the same area at a distance of about 2–3 miles from the parish. My predecessor used to say with some justification that you have to be a sheik or a vicar actually to live in the parish! – it is no longer quite as true as it was – but a number of people who had come to the church when they first moved to London either as students locally, (we live in the shadow of Imperial College and many Royal Colleges of this and that) or sharing a flat, had since got married and bought a house as close to the centre as they could afford, in Battersea or Clapham.

My predecessor, as vicar and area dean, wrote to the Bishop of the adjoining diocese the other side of the river and asked if ways could be looked at to enable an effective church plant into a nearly redundant building in his diocese to take place. It must be said that church planting wasn't very high on many Anglican agendas in this country then and probably because it has a threatening appearance, nothing really happened. Actually it took five years of discussion and correspondence before the Battersea plant took place.

In the meantime, an opportunity arose within our own diocese; the Bishop was extremely helpful; the parish was on its last legs and faced really with two alternatives: closure and death or a plant from a neighbouring church in a different deanery. It chose, after a careful consideration of the choice, which took longer than one might have expected, to receive the plant.

In 1985 therefore, the first plant took place and 100 people and a member of staff went off with the blessing of the Bishop and the sending congregation to start the new work. The number of people that went is larger than might be expected, but then the new building to which they were going was large and no one wanted to rattle around for long. Needless to say the excitement and enthusiasm was very effective and the new congregation grew steadily – it is now up to between 500–600 people and ready and keen itself to plant.

Meanwhile correspondence and discussions had continued with the diocese south of the river and in 1987 a group of 50 this time and a member of staff started in a church in the Kingston Area of the diocese of Southwark, with the blessing of the Bishop. I think it is true to say, and understandable, that the clergy of that area had considerable hesitations about the whole idea but, again, it has proved to be a great success. The congregation has grown steadily and relations with local churches are very good. So much so that the Bishop is keen to plant more from that "plant" and plans are going forward to that end.

The third time we planted was more complicated. Suffice it to say though, that St. Paul's Church in Onslow Square had been closed for 12 years and when, about six months after the Battersea plant it became clear that we were full again, we were able, again with the blessing and co-operation of the Diocesan authorities and the Bishop, to plant a new congregation there. It too is now flourishing, with several hundred people in the congregation, a large children's and family work and very active outreach to the community, AIDS work and social action. And now we're full again. I can only affirm the truth of the New Testament statement that "the more you give, the more you get"! And I'm equally sure that you only get in order that you should give and this process can be continued as long as the Lord allows.

In our view this particularly Anglican method of planting – with a church, a full-time member of staff and up to 50 people – is an excellent method and we have seen some of the results in terms of new members. We recently had a "re-union" in the Westminster Central Hall for the 2,000 people that are the present result of these plants! But I would hope that we can accelerate the process somewhat.

It *is* happening and signs are encouraging, but I have not made any secret of my longing to see it happen much more frequently and on a smaller scale with "lay" led leadership in addition to the rather fraught but immensely worthwhile model that I have outlined above. I'm sure we could do it. But I think we need to recognize and be grateful for the co-workers that God is raising up in all the other denominations and house/new churches. They are our friends and brethren and it seems to me that this next stage of the growth of the Kingdom is being planned by God for us all to do together, pooling vision, resources, manpower, buildings etc. That truly will require a fresh look at our priorities and our adaptability; but it will be fun!